UNVEILING the Kings of ISRAEL

UNVEILING THE KINGS OF ISRAEL

First printing: July 2011
Second printing: April 2012

Master Books®, P.O. Box 726, Green Forest, AR 72638

Master Books® is a division of the New Leaf Publishing Group, Inc.

ISBN-13: 978-0-89051-609-6
Library of Congress Catalog Number: 2011927776

Cover design by Diana Bogardus.
Interior design by Terry White.

All photos by David Down, shutterstock.com, and Wikimedia Commons.

Please consider requesting that a copy of this volume be purchased by your local library system.

Printed in China

Please visit our website for other great titles:

www.masterbooks.net

For information regarding author interviews, please contact the publicity department at (870) 438-5288

Master Books®
A Division of New Leaf Publishing Group
www.masterbooks.net

CONTENTS

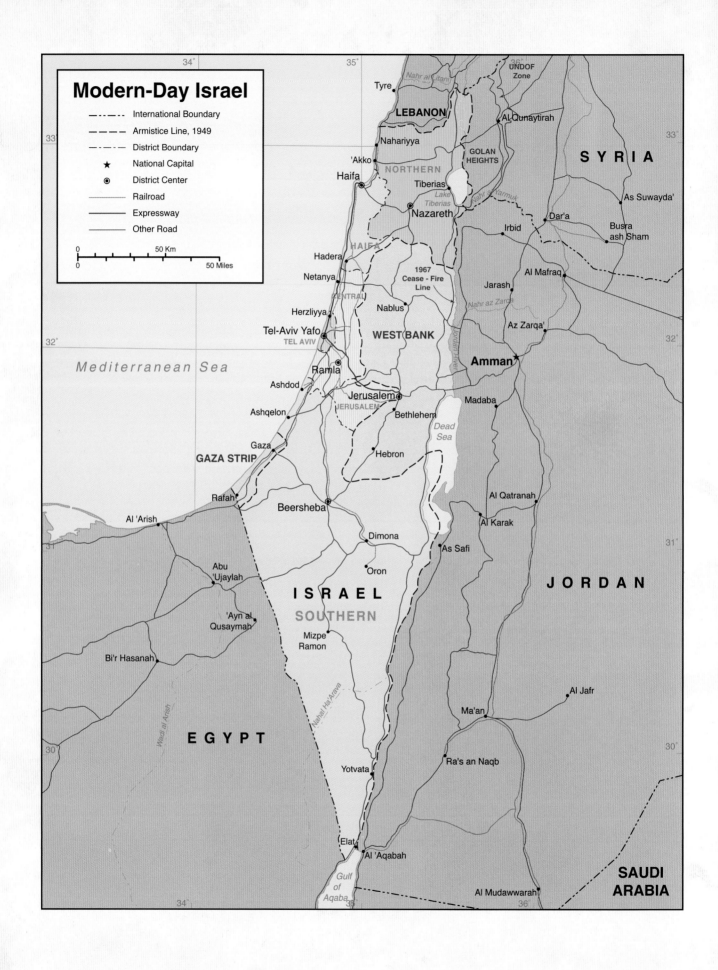

Modern-Day Israel

–·–·–·–	International Boundary
– – – –	Armistice Line, 1949
–··–··–	District Boundary
★	National Capital
◉	District Center
——	Railroad
——	Expressway
——	Other Road

Tyre

Nahr al Litani

LEBANON

UNDOF Zone

Al Qunaytirah

Nahariyya

NORTHERN

GOLAN HEIGHTS

SYRIA

'Akko

Haifa

Tiberias

Lake Tiberias

As Suwayda'

Nazareth

Nahr al Yarmuk

HAIFA

Irbid

Dar'a

Busra ash Sham

Hadera

1967 Cease - Fire Line

Al Mafraq

Netanya

CENTRAL

Jarash

Nahr az Zarqa

Herzliyya

Nablus

Az Zarqa'

Tel-Aviv Yafo

TEL AVIV

WEST BANK

Amman

Mediterranean Sea

Ramla

Ashdod

Jerusalem

JERUSALEM

Madaba

Ashqelon

Bethlehem

Dead Sea

Gaza

Hebron

GAZA STRIP

Al Qatranah

Rafah

Al Karak

Al 'Arish

Beersheba

Dimona

As Safi

JORDAN

Abu 'Ujaylah

Oron

ISRAEL

SOUTHERN

'Ayn al Qusaymah

Mizpe Ramon

Al Jafr

Bi'r Hasanah

EGYPT

Nahal Ha'Arava

Ma'an

Wadi al Arish

Yotvata

Ra's an Naqb

Elat

Al 'Aqabah

SAUDI ARABIA

Gulf of Aqaba

Al Mudawwarah

THE AUTHORITY OF THE BIBLE FACES A CRISIS. ITS HISTORICAL reliability is being challenged. Reputable archaeologists have written articles in magazines, and have appeared in television documentaries claiming that there is no evidence for the records of the Israelites leaving Egypt in the Exodus, for the conquest of Jericho and the invasion of Palestine by the incoming Israelites. They further point out that there is no archaeological evidence to support the Bible record of the reigns of David and Solomon, and that the Bible passages telling of the power and affluence of these kings are either totally wrong or greatly exaggerated. Based on the chronology usually ascribed to the history of Egypt, and the archaeological ages in Palestine, one might believe these are correct claims.

The chronological information in the Bible indicates that the Exodus would have occurred about 1445 BC. By the standard chronology of Egypt this would have been during the eighteenth dynasty of Egypt. This was a period of unparalleled power and prosperity. The movements of the Pharaohs and their armies are faithfully recorded. There is no trace of Israelite slave labor during this dynasty. There is no indication of a disaster striking the powerful Egyptian army at this time.

By the Bible chronology, the destruction of Jericho would have occurred about 1405 BC. At this time there is no evidence of fallen walls or a burnt city. If Jericho had been systematically and thoroughly burned as recorded in the Bible, archaeologists should be able to dig down in the ruins and find fallen walls and a layer of ash. There is no such evidence in this period.

The subsequent invasion of Palestine and its occupation by a new people would have occurred about the middle of the Late Bronze Period, but in this archaeological period there is no trace of a new people coming into the land.

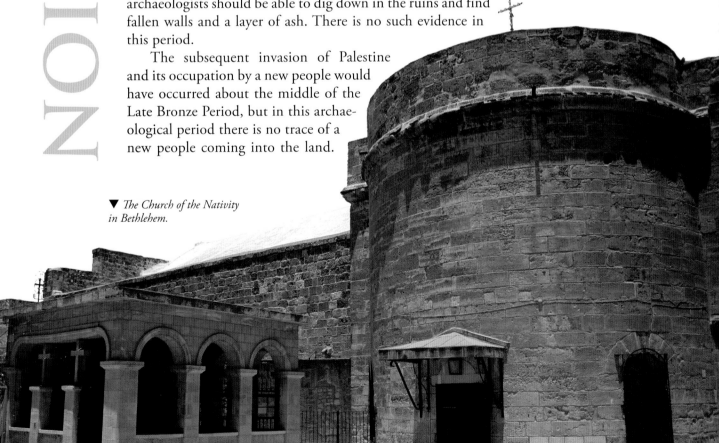

▼ *The Church of the Nativity in Bethlehem.*

If Israel occupied Palestine at this time, archaeologists should be able to find evidence of new pottery styles, ornaments of Egyptian origin, and different burial practices. Such evidence is entirely lacking.

Bible chronology would place David on the throne of Israel about 1010 BC. By archaeological reckoning this would be at the beginning of the Iron Age II Period. Archaeologists digging down into the ruins of biblical cities should be able to find strong walls, stone towers, ornate pottery, and expensive ornaments. Again, this evidence is lacking. In fact the Iron Age II period is one of abject poverty.

So what conclusions should we draw from all this? We are obliged to conclude that the historical records of the Bible are totally unreliable or that the usually accepted chronology is drastically misdated. The history of the kings of Israel as recorded in this book is based on the claim that the usually accepted chronology of Egypt and the archaeological strata in Israel have been grossly misdated. They need to be redated in some places by up to six hundred years. When this is done a remarkable synchronism can be found between the Bible records and the archaeological evidence. In dynasty twelve in Egypt there is evidence for the existence of large numbers of Semitic slaves who suddenly disappeared. In Israel at the beginning of the Middle Bronze Period there is evidence of a new people arriving and settling down all over the country. Archaeologists found walls in Jericho that had tilted over and a thick layer of ash that extended all over the stricken city. During the ensuing Middle Bronze Period there is abundant evidence of prosperity and power.

Archaeologists who cling to the traditional chronology challenge revisionists with fiddling with the dates, but an examination of the evidence upon which the traditional chronology is based reveals alarming inconsistencies. The traditional dates of Egyptian history have been largely based on the records of an Egyptian priest by the name of Manetho who left a list of dynasties and kings and their

Western Wall in the Old City of Jerusalem, the most important Jewish religious site with al-Aqsa mosque (right) and Dome of the Rock (left) in the background. ▼

lengths of reign. But Manetho lived in the third century BC after the dynasties of Egypt had come to an end. No one can be sure that his records are reliable. There is also the problem that his records do not exist anymore. We only know what he wrote because they were quoted by later historians but how can we be sure they quoted him correctly? We know that in some cases at least they did not quote him correctly because in several cases their records do not agree with each other.

Correctly interpreted the historical records of Egypt and Israel show a remarkable consistency with the Bible records, which we can accept as not only inspiring but also entirely reliable.

Excavations at Jericho by Dr Kathleen Kenyon. ▶

A GLOBAL FLOOD

Evidence and Fossils ▲   ▲ Depictions of Noah's ark

Chapter 1

MANKIND'S ANCESTORS

Thousands of years ago a world-wide flood engulfed this world. Only Noah and his family survived. From them the entire human race has descended. Evidence for this global catastrophe can be seen in the geological strata, which are exposed in road and railway cuttings, and in valley walls like the Grand Canyon of America. Cuneiform tablets called the Gilgamesh Epic were found in Nineveh in ancient Assyria. This record corresponds very closely with the biblical record. Contrary to claims that have been made by unqualified travelers, Noah's ark has never been found. There are many highly qualified scientists in the world who support the creation and flood record in the Bible.

GENESIS

THE MOST DEVASTATING CATASTROPHE THAT EVER HIT this world was the global deluge recorded in the Book of Genesis in the Bible. "The waters prevailed exceedingly on the earth, and all the high hills under the whole heaven were covered. The waters prevailed fifteen cubits upward, and the mountains were covered. And all flesh died that moved on the earth: birds and cattle and beasts and every creeping thing that creeps on the earth, and every man" (Gen. 7:19–21). Only Noah and his family survived in the huge boat that he had built.

This boat was a remarkable structure. Most translations call it an ark, and artists depict it in the shape of a modern boat, but the Hebrew word from which the word ark is translated literally means "box." Certainly the ark of the covenant (in which were preserved the Ten Commandments) was an oblong box (Exod. 25:10), and as Noah's ark did not need to cut through the water or go anywhere, it was probably rectangular in shape. But it was the size that was so staggering: 300 x 50 cubits (about 450 x 75 ft. or 135 x 22 m) (Gen. 6:15) — large enough to accommodate at least two of every kind of land vertebrate that had been created.

FOSSILS AND THE FLOOD

We do not have to look far for evidence that this Flood happened. The geological strata that were laid down after the Flood can be seen in railway and road cuttings through hills. Most geologists would have us believe that these layers of rock gradually accumulated over millions of years, but even a casual observer can see that these strata do not gradually merge into each other, as they would if gradual accumulation had occurred. In most cases there are sharp distinctions between the layers, demonstrating that they were deposited suddenly. No sooner had one layer been deposited than another was dumped on top of it, with no evidence of erosion in those so-called intervening eons.

Moreover, the presence of vast numbers of fossils in these layers provides convincing evidence that life was suddenly obliterated. Fossils are generally not forming today. Animals and fish that die slowly disintegrate. Fossils are usually well preserved, meaning they were suddenly buried. The waters of the Flood eroded and deposited layer upon layer of sand and mud in huge quantities all over the earth, entombing life. These layers soon hardened and turned into rock.

Evolutionists tell us that the strata were laid down over millions of years, burying the fossils as the debris accumulated, starting with the most primitive forms of life and ending with the latest life forms. If that were so, the earliest life forms would all be on the bottom layers and the latest forms on top, with the evolving forms of life ascending in progressive layers. But that is not the way it is.

The earliest fossils found in the rocks are anything but primitive. Every major body plan appeared "suddenly" in what has been called the "Cambrian explosion." There is no clue to what they could have evolved from. Furthermore, there should be countless transitional forms in the fossil record, but these are missing. And fossils

The Book of Genesis tells how God commanded Noah (a man of righteousness) to build the ark to save himself, his family, and the animals of the world from a worldwide flood that would destroy all life. ▼

▲ *The Grand Canyon in America is one mile deep and should be a geologist's dream.*

▲ *God created a rainbow as a promise to Noah that He would not flood the entire world again.*

▲ *Claims abound that parts of Noah's ark have been found around the mountains of Ararat in Turkey.*

show so little change over time that they can easily be identified with still-living animals. They are called "living fossils."

The Grand Canyon in America should be a geologist's dream. It is one mile deep with dozens of strata exposed. The earliest forms of life should be at the bottom and the evolving forms of life should be found in the successive layers. Unfortunately for the evolutionist, the fossils are not in that order.

As might be expected, most marine life is at the bottom, but as the layers rise there are numerous sections where whole systems of fossils are missing. Bizarre explanations about the whole continent sinking beneath the ocean and rising up again have been suggested to explain periods of deposition and periods of erosion, but the explanations tax the imagination. Actually, sea shells can be found on top of the world's highest mountains, a convincing testimony to the Bible statement that "all the high hills under the whole heaven were covered" (Gen. 7:19).

Some may wonder how there could have been so much water to cover all the high mountains, but mountains and hills might not have been as high as they are today. Toward the end of the Flood, lateral pressure would have squeezed the hills, thrusting them up to great heights. Since the Flood, volcanoes have belched forth lava that has piled volcanic mountains to lofty grandeur. All this is the result of the Flood. During the closing stages of the Flood, "the mountains rose, the valleys sank down" (Ps. 104:8; ESV). This psalm seems to refer to God's rainbow promise. Some ocean beds are deeper than the height of the loftiest mountains. Nearly three-quarters of the world's surface is covered by water. No need to wonder where the water of the Flood went. When the oceans sank down, water would have raced through the land, quickly carving valleys and ravines into the rain-soaked earth.

WHERE IS ARARAT?

There has been much speculation about Noah's ark. Expeditions to Turkey have claimed that the remains of his boat have been found on Mount Ararat. Actually, it is likely that the traditional Mount Ararat today was not formed until after the Flood. It is a volcanic mountain 16,916 feet (5,126 m) in height, and it was not named Mount Ararat until the Armenians became Christians in the third century A.D. They assumed that the highest mountain in the region must be Mount Ararat. The Turkish name for this mountain is Agri Darg.

On a smaller mountain near Agri Darg, called lesser Mount Ararat, is a ship-shaped object the size of Noah's ark that became the focus of a sensational claim. However, qualified geologists have identified it as a geological syncline. There are similar geological formations in the vicinity, some larger, some smaller, and they can't all be Noah's ark.

BIBLICAL ACCOUNT SUPPORTED

The Bible does not specifically say that the ark came to rest on Mount Ararat. It simply says that the ark came to rest "on the mountains of Ararat." Ararat was a country known to the Assyrians as Urartu, now Armenia. There are plenty of lofty mountain ranges in this area, any one of which could have been the mountain on which the ark came to rest. Whether the ark is still there or whether local peasants chopped it up for firewood long ago may never be known. The validity of the biblical record does not depend on the discovery of the ark.

However, strong support for the Bible account comes from archaeological discovery. Ashurbanipal, the last great king of the Assyrian empire, appreciated the importance of education. He built a library in his palace at Nineveh and amassed a huge collection of clay tablets. Some

25,000 tablets, or fragments of tablets, have been found.

The famous archaeologist Henry Austin Layard conducted excavations in Nineveh, and in 1850, the second year of his excavations, he discovered the famous library that had been gathered somewhere between 669 and 630 B.C.

Most of the tablets were inscribed in the Akkadian language in the cuneiform script that few scholars could read at that time, so when several crates of these tablets arrived at the British Museum they were simply stored away in a back room.

When the cuneiform script had been cracked by Henry Rawlinson, scholars began the enormous task of translating the tablets in the British Museum. George Smith was an enterprising young man involved in the task. One day in 1872 he was startled to pick up a tablet and read what seemed like the story of Noah and the Flood. His announcement of what he had found created enormous interest. So much so that the *London Daily Telegraph* offered him 1,000 pounds sterling to go to Ashurbanipal's palace in Nineveh and search for the missing parts of the story. Finding the proverbial needle in a haystack would have seemed less impossible, but the dauntless George accepted the challenge and set off.

Then the unbelievable happened. Within a week of his arrival in Nineveh, George Smith dug out another cache of tablets, among them a further 11 pieces dealing with the Flood story. There were still some missing parts, but when the finds were made public all scholars agreed that the story, which came to be known as *The Epic of Gilgamesh*, was the Assyrian version of the Flood story as told in the Bible (Gen. 6–9).

Here are some of the relevant portions of the famous *Epic of Gilgamesh*:

Gilgamesh I will reveal unto thee a hidden thing, Shuruppak, a city that thou knowest, and which now lies in ruins on the banks of the Euphrates; when that city was old and there were yet gods within it, the gods decided to bring on a deluge. Their father Anu, repeated the words: Lord of Shuruppak, son of Ubar-Tutu, destroy thy house

ANCIENT SUPERSHIPS

Many people discount the possible construction of ships as large as the ark in Noah's time, but there have been archaeological references to other ancient superships in the Mediterranean (Greece and Roman) and even Asia (China specifically).

and build a vessel! Abandoning riches do thou seek out living kind, despising possessions, preserve what has life: thus load in the vessel the seed of all creatures.

When something of morning dawned, I commanded that the land be assembled . . . for four days were gathered the parts of the vessel — the boys fetching pitch, while the stronger brought timber-materials. I made enter the vessel all my family and kindred; beasts wild and

▼ *One of 12 clay tablets containing a portion of* The Epic of Gilgamesh, *poetry from Mesopotamia, and among the earliest known works of literature. The story tells of a great flood similar to the deluge of Noah's day.*

domestic.

Came the set time appointed: who was sending the bane . . . did pour down the rain. For six days and seven nights the wind blew, and the flood and the storm swept the land . . . the whole of mankind had returned unto clay.

When I looked out again in the directions across the expanse of the sea, mountain ranges had emerged in twelve places and on Mount Nisir the vessel had grounded.

On the seventh's day arriving, I freed a dove. Forth went the dove but came back to me. Then I set free a swallow and did release him. Forth went the swallow but came back to me. So I set free a raven and did release him. Forth went the raven and he saw again the natural flowing of the waters and he ate and he flew about and he croaked and he came not returning.

So I set free all to the four winds and I poured a libation and scattered a food offering on the height of the mountain. And the gods smelled the savour, the gods smelled the sweet savour, the gods gathered like flies about the priests of the offering. Has ought of living kind escaped? Not a man should have survived the destruction.[1]

A comparison with Bible texts in Genesis shows a close parallel:

So the Lord said, "I will destroy man whom I have created from the face of the earth, both man and beast, creeping thing and birds of the air" (Gen. 6:7).

Make yourself an ark of gopherwood; make rooms in the ark, and cover it inside and outside with pitch (Gen. 6:14).

Of every living thing of all flesh you shall bring two of every sort into the ark (Gen. 6:19).

It came to pass after seven days that the waters of the flood were on the earth . . . . And the rain was on the earth forty days and forty nights (Gen. 7:10–12).

All in whose nostrils was the breath of the spirit of life, all that was on the dry land, died (Gen. 7:22).

So He destroyed all living things which were on the face of the ground; both man and cattle, creeping thing and bird of the air (Gen. 7:23).

---

1.   D. Winton Thomas, editor, *Documents from Old Testament Times* (New York: Harper and Rowe, 1958).

LOCATION OF ARARAT

There are two Mount Ararats - greater and lesser Ararat but they are both volcanic mountains and volcanoes would have come after the flood. They were given these names by the Armenians who lived in the area in the third century AD when they accepted Christianity as their state religion.

Then the ark rested in the seventh month, the seventeenth day of the month, on the mountains of Ararat (Gen. 8:4).

At the end of forty days . . . he sent out a raven, which kept going to and fro until the waters had dried up from the earth (Gen. 8:6–7).

He also sent out from himself a dove, to see if the waters had receded from the face of the ground. But the dove found no resting place for the sole of her foot, and she returned into the ark (Gen. 8:8–9).

Then Noah built an altar to the LORD, and took of every clean animal and of every clean bird, and offered burnt offerings on the altar. And the LORD smelled a soothing aroma (Gen. 8:20–21).

▼   *Sacrifice of Noah by Martinelli.*

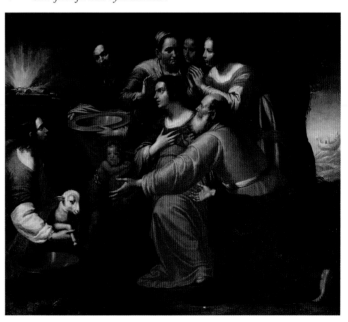

It has been argued that the Bible story is just an adaptation of the Gilgamesh legend, but it is significant that there are traces of the Flood and creation stories in the legends of many of the earth's nations: Chinese, Indian, Maori, and Australian Aborigine, to mention just a few. This points to the concept of mankind having one common source, and the resultant legends are just different versions of the same event, distorted by time and retelling.

▲ *Nineveh. The Mashki Gate. Reconstructed. One of the fifteen gateways of ancient Nineveh. The lower portions of the stone retaining wall are original. The gateway structure itself was originally of mudbrick. A few orthostats can be seen at the right of the passageway.*

An Encounter with History!

The historical account of Noah's ark has caught the interest of scholars and adventurers since antiquity. Even the question of a global flood is in dispute by those who reject a biblical worldview of history – despite scientific evidence which supports this perspective. From trying to determine the exact location of the "mountains of Ararat" to actual searches for physical remains of the ship, the ark has been a cautionary tale, a symbol of hope, a mystery, and even a point of contention over whether or not it could have really been built and survived a global flood. Doubt over the issue has been a stumbling block in the faith of many in the face of secular skepticism.

Results of a study by a ship research center provided some interesting results. "The study confirmed that the proportions of the ark were cleverly balanced – a taller ark might capsize, a longer one might break, and a wider or shorter ark could give a dangerously rough ride."[2]

Archaeological evidence has proven that shipbuilding has been taking place since the earliest civilizations, and examples of large wooden vessels are noted throughout history. Proportionally, it even appears the ark is similar to modern cargo ships. But that still leaves the question – could a ship this large be built of wood before the invention of steel and other modern shipbuilding techniques?

The creative team behind a new historically-themed attraction is about to answer the question by building a full-scale wooden ark replica in Kentucky (USA). The structure will be the centerpiece of the planned Ark Encounter project to officially open in 2014.

NOAH'S ARK
depicted through the years

▲ An unknown 13th-century Jewish artist designed this image of Noah's ark landing on the "Mountains of Ararat." (North French Hebrew Miscellany)

▲ The Deluge the Ark of Noah Drifting on the Water (Illustrator Petrus Comestors Bible Historials France, 1372).

▲ Construction of the Ark. (Scanned from Nuremberg Chronicle, 1493.)

▲ A painting by the American Edward Hicks (1780–1849), showing the animals boarding Noah's ark two by two.

The Ark, J&F Tallis London Edinburgh Dublin (The Complete Works of Flavius Josephus, 1845). ▶

Deluge painting by Bill Looney (The True Story of Noah's Ark, 2003). ▶

THE RISE OF UR

Tower of Babel ▲   ▲ Ur of the Chaldeans

Chapter 2

ABRAHAM CAME FROM UR

As Noah's descendants multiplied, a dissident group abandoned their mountain home and migrated down the Euphrates River and built a tower to enable them to survive any future deluge. God intervened by confusing their language and they were obliged to move to other areas. One group migrated downstream and established a settlement at a place which became known as Ur of the Chaldees. The Bible says Abraham and his family came from Ur. Sir Leonard Woolley excavated at Ur and found that it had been a remarkably advanced civilization.

NOW THE WHOLE EARTH HAD ONE LANGUAGE AND one speech. And it came to pass, as they journeyed from the east, that they found a plain in the land of Shinar and they dwelt there (Gen. 11:1–2).

As time went by, Noah's family increased and it was inevitable that a faction would develop that would become disgruntled with the traditional way of life and decide to go its own rebellious way. It is logical to assume that Mount Ararat was somewhere near the source of the river Euphrates and that this group followed this river down to the land of Shinar. At first the Euphrates flows in a westerly direction so they would have "journeyed from the east."

BABEL AND THE TOWER

Rebellious as the people were, they could not deny that there had been a huge Flood, and their guilty consciences told them that their rebellion could be visited with another disaster, so "they said to one another, 'Come, let us make bricks and bake them thoroughly.' They had brick for stone, and they had asphalt for mortar. And they said, 'Come, let us build ourselves a city, and a tower whose top is in the heavens" (Gen. 11:3–4).

This biblical record has a ring of authenticity to it. Moses was never in Babylon. He had come from Egypt where buildings were built with stone, and blocks of stone were sometimes cemented together with lime plaster. He obviously felt that some elucidation was called for to explain this building procedure that was unknown in Egypt. Archaeology has revealed that these towers were made of millions of fired bricks stuck together with asphalt.

For a long time it was thought that Birs Nimrud was the Tower of Babel. There are 32 known ziggurats, or temple towers, in Mesopotamia and Iran, and Birs Nimrud was the tallest and best preserved of them all. It was a huge mountain of thoroughly baked bricks that were stuck together with asphalt, of which there is no shortage in Iraq.

However, when Professor Koldewey excavated Babylon (1899–1917) he unearthed the foundations of an even larger ziggurat. But why were only the foundations of the original structure found? Over the centuries the temple tower had fallen into disrepair, so when Alexander the Great occupied Babylon after he returned from his great military campaign, which took him as far as India, his builders advised him that it would be better to dismantle the ziggurat and completely rebuild it. The ziggurat was dismantled, but before it could be rebuilt Alexander died and the ziggurat was never reconstructed.

The Bible words "Babel" and "Babylon" are both translated from the Hebrew consonants "BBL" (there are no vowels in the Hebrew

The site of Borsippa Iraq now called Birs Nimrud. The ziggurat, the "Tongue Tower," today one of the most vividly identifiable surviving ziggurats, is identified in the Talmud and Arab culture with the Tower of Babel. ▼

▲ *Close up of the rockwork from the ziggurat at Birs Nimrud. Bitumen (a tarlike, sticky, organic mixture that compares to asphalt) was used to bind and waterproof the bricks.*

▲ *The top of the ziggurat's tower once thought to be the remains of the Tower of Babel.*

alphabet), so they are one and the same thing. The Tower of Babel was the tower of Babylon and so should logically be found in Babylon.

CONSTRUCTION ENDS

The pride-driven Babel project was doomed to failure, and God brought the construction to an end in an interesting way. Up until then everyone spoke the same language, but "the Lord confused the language of all the earth" (Gen. 11:9). When they could not understand each other's speech the work came to an abrupt halt, and the different language groups migrated to other areas. Noah had three sons: Shem, Ham, and Japheth. Shem's descendants became the Semitic nations: Hebrews, Arabs, Assyrians, Elamites, and Syrians. Ham became the progenitor of the Canaanites, Egyptians, and Africans, and Japheth was the father of the nations of the rest of the world.

One group that moved away from Babylon became known as the Sumerians, whose capital city was Ur in southern Iraq. It seems likely they became the earliest civilization in the world, even ahead of Egypt. They invented cuneiform writing and developed a remarkable knowledge of mathematics and geometry.

It took a long time for the Sumerians to be identified. In the whole of the Bible, there are only four references to Ur of the Chaldees, and all of them refer to the same event: Abram (his original name) leaving Ur. Typical of these references is Genesis 11:31, where the Bible says, "And Terah took his son Abram and his grandson Lot, the son of Haran, and his daughter-in-law Sarai, his son Abram's wife, and they went out with them from Ur of the Chaldees to go to the land of Canaan."

In southern Iraq there is a very interesting ziggurat, or temple tower, known to the local people as Tell el Muqayyar, meaning Mound of Pitch, so named because the bricks of

the ziggurat are stuck together with bitumen or pitch. The ruins were obviously important, but what was it? What city had been here? What nation was responsible for this great edifice? These questions went unanswered for a long time.

SHROUDED BY TIME

In the year 1854, the British Museum approached the foreign office with a request that the British representative in Iraq be commissioned to search for treasures to grace the museum. The foreign office obligingly communicated the request to the British consul in Basra, J. E. Taylor. This good man was not, of course, an archaeologist, nor had he any experience with excavations, but he was a willing servant of Her Majesty's government and no doubt welcomed a break from his office routines. Rounding up a caravan of camels and donkeys laden with picks, hoes, and supplies, he set out for Tell el Muqayyar. After all, what better place to start his digging than the well-known Mound of Pitch?

Arriving at the lonely desert site approximately 93 miles (150 km) northwest of Basra, he made an inspection of the mighty ziggurat. Carefully tapping on the brick walls, he listened for any echo that would betray a hollow place within. There was none. The edifice was as solid as the Rock of Gibraltar. Undaunted, Taylor set his men to work on the top of the building. He was still convinced that somewhere inside this giant temple there must be stored fabulous treasures that he could recover and proudly dispatch to London.

The Arab laborers obediently began their task, levering bricks from their place and hurling them to the ground below. The great temple tower that had withstood the ravages of thousands of years of heat, wind, and driving sand began to yield to the onslaughts of ignorant humanity.

But if Taylor had visions of graceful stone statues or golden gods, he was doomed to disappointment. After two

▲ *A relief of Akhenaten, Nefertiti, and their children. For a short time under Akhenaten's rule Egypt was considered monotheistic, though this was rare at that time.*

years of wearisome toil, all he could send back to London were four small clay barrels covered with mysterious cuneiform characters, which his men had recovered from the corners of the ziggurat. The directors of the British Museum were equally disappointed. After the spectacular discoveries from Nineveh by Henry Layard, this was indeed an anticlimax. Little did they realize the inestimable value of the finds that Taylor had made.

THE EXISTENCE OF UR

When these cylinders were finally translated it was found that they had been inserted in the corner of the building as foundation stones by Nabonidus, last king of Babylon, who had rebuilt the ziggurat. Nabonidus's mother had been a priestess of the moon god Nannar in her hometown of Haran, and Nabonidus was naturally a devotee of this deity. As the ziggurat at Tell el Muqayyar was dedicated to the moon god Nannar and his wife Ningal, Nabonidus had taken an interest in the restoration of the tower.

On the cylinder he referred to the king who had first erected the ziggurat. This king's name, according to Nabonidus, was Ur-Nammu. Ur-Nammu? Could it be that

this king's name was Nammu and he was the king of Ur? To think that here was the original home of the great patriarch Abram was an exciting prospect indeed. Time was to prove that the guess was correct, and this great temple tower was at the heart of a thriving metropolis, the capital city of a great empire and a highly developed civilization that actually predated the great Egyptian civilization.

In the meantime, apart from the local builders who saw in the age-old bricks that Taylor's men had pried free a ready source of building materials, Tell el Muqayyar was forgotten. The stately temple tower sank back to its desert solitude.

A SECOND LOOK AT UR

The year was 1918 and the great world war was drawing to a close. The Turks were driven out of the Euphrates Valley and the British army was in control. One of the British officers in the area was Major R. Campbell Thompson, attached to the intelligence staff of the army, and he was stationed near Tell el Muqayyar. It so happened that in private life before the war started, Thompson had been an assistant in the British Museum. He took more than a casual interest in the towering ziggurat and the telltale mounds surrounding it. In fact, as opportunity provided, he did a little excavating on the spot. He was impressed with what he found and sent a recommendation back to the British Museum that it would be worth mounting a full-scale expedition to this place.

In response to Major Thompson's advice, the British Museum commissioned Dr. H. R. Hall to proceed to the site and commence excavations. He arrived late in 1918 and made some experimental soundings at Tell el Muqayyar and also at some nearby sites, Eridu and Al Ubaid. The latter revealed that they were looking at what could prove to be the world's earliest civilization. Lack of adequate funds curtailed further digging, but they had done enough to demonstrate that further excavations were more than warranted.

In 1922 the University of Pennsylvania approached the British Museum with the suggestion that a joint expedition be mounted, and the British accepted the suggestion. Charles Leonard Woolley, later to be knighted for his outstanding work in the field, was placed in charge of the expedition. The 43-year-old Woolley had already proven his worth in excavations in Egypt and Carchemish, and his work showed that he was ideally suited for the assignment. He virtually made it his life work and for the next 12 years toiled patiently at the site. His wife also worked with him much of the time.

Woolley's excavation revealed that the people of Ur were a highly intelligent and well-educated people. Their arts were well developed and they traded with countries far removed from them. Some semi-precious stones of which their ornaments were made came from the Nilgiri Hills in southern India.

A THRIVING, ADVANCED CITY

A central feature of the city of Ur was the ziggurat, or temple tower. This, and the surrounding temple complex, probably had its beginning in the first dynasty. But it was enlarged and beautified by Ur-Nammu of the third dynasty, which

 Babylonian stone with religious images and cuneiform writing.

THE RELIGION OF ABRAHAM

We know nothing of Abraham's religion apart from the Bible record. Monotheism was unknown at this time. Abraham worshipped an invisible God; therefore, there were no objects of worship left as relics with which to discover and study.

carried Ur to the zenith of its power. Houses during this and subsequent periods were of remarkably good quality.

The rich possessed well-built double-story homes that were built around an inner court. A curious feature of many houses of Ur was the drainage system. A shaft up to 30 or more feet (10 m) deep was dug and a series of pottery rings was inserted. This shaft then became a very effective soak-pit for the family's wastes. In fact, the drainage system was a lot better than the systems found in most of the homes in Iraq today.

Scholarship in Ur was of a remarkably high standard. Woolley wrote the following in his very readable book, *The Sumerians*:

> Many school tablets survive and illustrate the course of study practiced in the temple classes. First there are long lists of single signs with their phonetic values for the pupil to memorize, then lists of signs grouped together in alphabetical order, and of ideograms, the signs which stood for a single word or idea and might be inserted in the text before a compound group to give its generic meaning in advance. . . . Then some short sentences, the common formulae of texts, honorific titles, and so on, and from these the pupil advanced to the grammar of the language and we find tablets giving the paradigms of verbs and the declension of nouns. By this time he was writing on his own account. On one side of a flat round tablet of soft clay the teacher wrote his "fair copy" and the learner, after studying this, turned the tablet over and endeavored to reproduce on the back of it what had been written.
>
> After grammar came mathematics, and we find tables of multiplication and division, tables for the

▲ *Excavated ruins in the town of Ur, in southern Iraq with a ziggurat in the background.*

ANCIENT DEITIES AND TODAY

Did the worship of various nature deities of that time — like the moon god — influence the cultures of today? Sin was the name given the moon god and Nannar was his wife. Ishtar was the Babylonian fertility god, from which we get the word "Easter." Ashtoreth was the Hebrew equivalent of this name.

extraction of square and cube roots, and exercises in applied geometry — for instance, how to calculate the area of a plot of ground of irregular shape by squaring it off so that the total of the complete squares included in it added to that of the right-angled triangles which fill in its contours gives an answer approximately correct; then there are lists of weights and measures, and for those whose studies had a more scholarly purpose there are introduced towards the end of our period dictionaries in which Sumerian and Semitic synonyms are given in parallel columns.[1]

How Abram's father Terah came to be in Ur is not disclosed, but he was there. In Ur was the large ziggurat dedicated to the moon god Nannar, and Terah apparently became contaminated with this pagan worship, but Abram had loftier concepts of God. So "the Lord had said to Abram: 'Get out of your country, from your family and from your father's house, to a land that I will show you'" (Gen. 12:1).

Terah accepted the challenge and "took his son Abram and his grandson Lot, the son of Haran, and his daughter-in-law Sarai, his son Abram's wife, and they went out with them from Ur of the Chaldeans to go to the land of Canaan; and they came to Haran and dwelt there" (Gen. 11:31).

Today Haran is only a small village in southeast Turkey, but in early times it was an important city on the trade route from the Persian Gulf to the Mediterranean.

1.   C. Leonard Woolley, *The Sumerians* (New York: W.W. Norton, 1965), p. 109–110.

LIFE IN A HAREM

What would Sarai's life have been like in a harem? Wives lived in a separate building and would have had maidservants. Life would have been easy, comfortable, and even luxurious. They would have few marital duties. Sarah would have found it more attractive than living in a tent.

MOON WORSHIP

Ya'acov Shkolnik wrote an article about Haran in *Eretz,* Israel's geographic magazine, that he entitled "Moon capital of Mesopotamia." He wrote, "The present-day village has slipped into relative anonymity, and covers a much smaller area than that of the ancient city. But in antiquity, Haran was an important community."[2]

To the Egyptians, the sun was the most evident manifestation of the deity, but to the people of Mesopotamia the moon had a much stronger appeal. "The sun always looked the same, while the moon changed form. Its magical power stemmed from its ability to regenerate itself."[3] By the moon the months were measured, it changed shape, and "more than any other celestial body, it was a living creature. It was born, grew, died, and was reborn."[4]

▲ *A painting depicting the Babylonian marriage market by the nineteenth-century artist Edwin Long.*

Why Abraham did not immediately proceed to Canaan is not stated. Perhaps Terah had ill health, for "he died in Haran" (Gen. 11:32). Abram tarried no longer in this center of idolatrous moon worship and, with his large retinue of servants and huge flocks of sheep and goats, continued to follow the course of the Euphrates valley to Syria and then proceeded south to the land of Canaan.

Abram was no ignorant peasant. He was a wealthy chieftain who came from a cultured society. In fact, when he arrived in Egypt he had dealings with the pharaoh, who appropriated his wife Sarah into his harem (Gen. 12:15). The Jewish historian Josephus claimed, "He communicated to them arithmetic, and delivered to them the science of astronomy; for before Abram came into Egypt they were unacquainted with those parts of learning; for that science came from the Chaldeans into Egypt."[5]

Critics may dispute the reliability of this statement by Josephus, but it is significant that he should refer to such information when he would have had no way of knowing what we know today — that Ur was such an advanced seat of learning.

2. Ya'acov Shkolnik, "Moon capital of Mesopotamia," *Eretz* (March 2002): p. 35.
3. Ibid., p. 35.
4. Ibid., p. 135.
5. Flavius Josephus, *Antiquities of the Jews*, 1, VIII, 2.

SEED OF THE PROMISE

Reaching Haran ▲   ▲ Death in Hebron

Chapter 3

ABRAHAM IN CANAAN

When Abram's father Terah died, Abram and his large contingent crossed the Euphrates River and migrated to Shechem in the Promised Land. From there he proceeded to the Negev in the south, and because of a severe drought they migrated to Egypt. On his return from Egypt Abraham settled in Hebron. His nephew Lot chose to live in Sodom, which was subsequently destroyed by fire and brimstone. At Sarah's suggestion Abraham married her servant Hagar who gave birth to Ishmael, the progenitor of the Arab nations. Subsequently Sarah gave birth to a son called Isaac. When Sarah died she was buried in a cave in Hebron.

WHEN HIS FATHER TERAH DIED, ABRAM WAS ABLE TO continue his migration. "So Abram departed as the LORD had spoken to him, and Lot went with him. And Abram was seventy-five years old when he departed from Haran. Then Abram took Sarai his wife and Lot his brother's son, and all their possessions that they had gathered, and the people whom they had acquired in Haran, and they departed to go to the land of Canaan. So they came to the land of Canaan" (Gen. 12:4–5)

This addition to Abram's retinue may have come from his expanding wealth or it may have been as a result of conversions to his religion. Whichever it was, the large tribe would have crossed the Euphrates — not an easy task but they had done it before to reach Haran — and slowly made their way south through Syria to Shechem in the Promised Land.

A CHRONOLOGY CLUE

"Abram was seventy-five years old when he departed from Haran" (Gen. 12:4). This information provides us with a date for Abram's birth. First Kings 6:1 tells us, "In the four hundred and eightieth year after the children of Israel had come out of the land of Egypt, in the fourth year of Solomon's reign over Israel, in the month of Ziv, which is the second month, that he began to build the house of the LORD."

Solomon's accession year is usually placed about 969 B.C., so the fourth year of his reign would be 966 B.C. The 480th year before that would give the date of the Exodus as about 1445 B.C. Exodus 12:41 informs us, "At the end of the four hundred and thirty years — on that very same day — it came to pass that all the armies of the Lord went out from the land of Egypt." Galatians 3:17 indicates that this period is to be dated from the covenant made with Abram, giving us a date of 1875 B.C. for his departure from Haran, and his birth in Ur would have been about 1950 B.C.

The land of Canaan would have been a welcome change from the blistering plains of Mesopotamia. Shechem is pleasantly located between two lofty mountains — Gerizim and Ebal. Today it is on the perimeter of the expanding Muslim city of Nablus. It was first excavated by a German team from 1913 intermittently onward to 1934. In 1956 an American team under the respected archaeologist G. Ernest Wright began excavations that showed that when Abraham first went there, Shechem was only an unfortified village.

It was in Shechem that "the Lord appeared to Abram and said, 'To your descendents I will give this land." Encouraged by this divine promise, "He built an altar to the Lord, who had appeared to him" (Gen. 12:7).

But "the Canaanites were then in the land" (Gen. 12:6), and they may not have looked with favor on this large contingent that had arrived in their valley. Abram may have sensed some hostility and decided to move on and continue his journey south, passing by Bethel and proceeding to the Negev in

Standard of Ur "War" panel. ▼

▲ *Pyramids in Gizeh, Egypt, near sunset.*

▲ *Coastline of the Dead Sea, known also as the Salt Sea because of its heavy salinity.*

the south. The Negev is the area south of Beersheba and it has a very low rainfall. It is rather barren at any time, but when Abram arrived "there was a famine in the land" (Gen. 12:10). Abram would not have been impressed with his promised land and decided to move into Egypt.

This was a drastic step to take. Whichever route he followed he would have had to trudge through up to 62 miles (100 km) of barren, sandy desert. With large flocks to feed and water en route, that would have been a formidable assignment, but he made it.

INFLUENCING EGYPT

A stranger in a strange country, Abram was apprehensive about his beautiful wife, Sarai, and palmed her off as his sister. Actually, she *was* his half sister, but that still made it only a half truth. Sure enough, Pharaoh's scouts spotted the good-looking Sarai, and his princes also noticed her good looks. Sarai must have been very well preserved because she was 65 years of age when she was inducted into Pharaoh's harem.

Financially it seemed to be a good move for Abram. Pharaoh "treated Abram well for her sake. He had sheep, oxen, male donkeys, male and female servants, female donkeys, and camels" (Gen. 12:16).

No doubt Abram could have expected a generous dowry from Pharaoh for his beautiful sister, but it seems rather lavish even for such a prospective bride. There may have been more involved than the Bible record spells out. A look at the political circumstances in Egypt at this time may hold the clue.

By the traditional chronology of Egypt this would have happened during the 12th or 13th dynasties, but by the reduced chronology I have supported in my book *Unwrapping the Pharaohs*,[1] Abram's visit would have been during Dynasty 4. This would then agree with the statement by the Jewish historian Josephus, who wrote that "he communicated to them arithmetic, and delivered to them the science of astronomy; for before Abram came into Egypt they were unacquainted with those parts of learning; for that science came from the Chaldeans into Egypt."[2]

The biggest pyramid in Egypt was built by Khufu and is a masterpiece of engineering. It is exactly square, exactly level at the base, exactly orientated to the four points of the compass, and, taking the height of the pyramid as the radius of a circle, the circumference of the circle would be exactly equal to the perimeter of the base. This is either a remarkable coincidence or it means that the Egyptians had suddenly discovered the use of the formula 2PR. It may well be that it was Abram who taught them and Pharaoh was impressed enough to lavish his gifts on Abram.

So the liaison between Abram and the pharaoh may have been closer than previously suggested, though it was a cowardly lack of faith on Abram's part to palm his wife off as his sister. But God showed him mercy by plaguing Pharaoh and his household, and Pharaoh became aware of the deceit. He gave Abram a sharp rebuke and returned his wife to him before he had opportunity to defile her. He said, "Why did you say, 'She is my sister'? I might have taken her as my wife" (Gen. 12:19).

LEAVING EGYPT

Once more crossing the arid desert, Abram returned to the Negev and then on to Bethel. Here his nephew's herdsmen had a dispute with Abram's staff and Abram nobly gave Lot the choice of location. Lot chose the plain of Sodom, and Abram remained on the plateau.

Following this noble gesture the Lord spoke to Abram and promised him that he would inherit the land of Canaan: "I will make your descendants as the dust of the

1.   John Ashton and David Down, *Unwrapping the Pharaohs* (Green Forest, AR: Master Books, 2006).

2.   Flavius Josephus, *Antiquities of the Jews*, I. VIII. 2.

▲ *Abraham's Departure, by József Molnár (1850).*

surprise attack, defeated the invaders and recovered his nephew Lot (Gen. 14:14–16).

GOD'S PROMISE KEPT

When Abraham was 99 years of age, God changed his name from Abram, meaning "Exalted Father," to Abraham, which possibly means "Father of a Multitude." God also required Abraham to circumcise all the males in his household as a token of their covenant relationship with God (Gen. 17:10–14). Abraham would have been familiar with this ritual, which was practiced in Egypt. Most royal mummies show evidence of circumcision. God also changed Sarai's name from Sarai, which can mean a dominant person, to Sarah, which can be translated queen, as in Isaiah 49:23.

God had promised to make Abraham's descendants into a great nation, but at that time he had none. Naturally, Abraham was concerned that Sarah, his wife, was barren. Abraham had his share of concubines (Gen. 25:6), but their children could not inherit his title. So at Sarah's suggestion, he took matters into his own hands and married her servant Hagar, who bore him a son whom he called Ishmael, meaning "God hears" (Gen. 16:11). This move was destined to bring trouble to the world until the end of time. Ishmael became the progenitor of the Arab nations with whom Israel is in a perpetual state of friction.

One day Abraham was sitting at the door of his tent when three well-dressed men approached. Abraham hastened to greet them and invited them to enjoy his hospitality. They accepted his offer and Abraham instructed Sarah to prepare some food. It was not appropriate for a woman to appear in public, but Sarah would have been keen to know who these men were. After organizing her servants to prepare the meal, Sarah pressed close to the flap of the tent to hear what was being said. What she heard electrified her.

"Sarah your wife shall have a son," one of the men said. Sarah could not suppress her contemptuous mirth. Have a child at her age? But it was the Lord Himself in human garb who had said this and He asked, "Why did Sarah laugh. . . ? Is anything too hard for the Lord?" (Gen. 18:10–14).

In due time Sarah did give birth to a son, whom Abraham appropriately called *Yitschaq,* a Hebrew word

earth" (Gen. 13:16). This was a remarkable promise since Abram had no children by Sarai at this time and she was already beyond child-bearing age. He subsequently moved south to Hebron.

While Abraham was in Hebron, four kings from Mesopotamia came with their armies and put the country to tribute. In the 14th year, the local nations rebelled against this domination so the four kings returned. A battle was fought and the Mesopotamian kings were victorious and plundered Sodom and Gomorrah, even taking Lot captive.

"Now the valley of Siddim was full of asphalt pits, and the kings of Sodom and Gomorrah fled; some fell there, and the remainder fled to the mountains" (Gen. 14:10). There are still many asphalt pits in the Dead Sea valley and they are treacherous. They form under the surface of the ground, and the earth above them can suddenly collapse under pressure. Apparently some of the fleeing kings fell into these pits.

Lot was a captive, but Abram was not powerless against the invaders. An indication of Abram's possessions can be inferred from the fact that besides his family and other retainers he had "three hundred and eighteen trained servants" (Gen. 14:14). There would have been more than 1,000 people in his tribe. He set out in pursuit and, in a

THE END OF LOT'S WIFE

If you look closer at the word "became" in Genesis 19:26, it may also hold a clue to what happened to Lot's wife. In Egypt it was noted that Israel "became" a great nation (Deut. 26:5), though this did not happen overnight. It may well have taken time for Lot's wife to "become" a pillar of salt as the sulfurous fumes over took her.

meaning "he laughs." So the name of Isaac immortalized the incident.

WICKED CITIES DESTROYED

Sodom and Gomorrah were twin cities in the region of the Dead Sea that had become corrupted with wealth and immorality. "And the LORD said, 'Shall I hide from Abraham what I am doing?'" (Gen. 18:17). It was His intention to destroy Sodom, and the two angels in human form departed on their deadly mission and to warn Lot as well.

Lot seems to have been a city official, and he was sitting in the city gateway where the business of the city was transacted. When two distinguished visitors approached, Lot extended to them his hospitality and they all retired to his home.

But some of the corrupt residents of Sodom had also taken note of the good-looking visitors, and after nightfall they surrounded Lot's house and demanded that the two men be handed over to them to indulge their lusts. It was only the angels exercising supernatural power that protected them from such indignities. The angels also announced their intention to destroy Sodom and advised Lot to warn his family members to flee from the doomed city, but his sons-in-law scoffed at his fears.

When the morning dawned, the angels urged Lot to take his wife and two daughters and flee from the city, saying, "Escape for your life! Do not look behind you nor stay anywhere in the plain" (Gen. 19:17).

A DEADLY CONSEQUENCE

Lot and his wife and two daughters fled, but Lot's wife could not resist the temptation to stop and look back at her beloved home. The delay proved fatal. "She became a pillar of salt" (Gen. 19:26).

This consequence may not have been instantaneous. "The Lord rained brimstone and fire on Sodom and Gomorrah" (Gen. 19:24). Fire would have been red-hot volcanic ash. Not far away is the Syrian desert, which is strewn with volcanic boulders, no doubt from this eruption. The brimstone was sulfur found in abundance in the Dead Sea region. In fact, there is now a sulfur factory at the south end of the Dead Sea that exports tons of the chemical.

The sulfurous fumes may well have been rolling out of Sodom and, as with Pompeii, asphyxiating all in their path. These fumes may have caught up with Lot's wife, and anything that is immobilized in that area becomes a pillar of salt. The Dead Sea is 25 percent salt and the atmosphere is literally saturated with salt. On the cliffs on the western side of the Dead Sea is a prominent pillar that has been called "Lot's wife," but it is simply rock salt and has nothing to do with Lot's wife.

Sodom and Gomorrah have never been identified. For many years it was thought they may have been beneath the shallow waters at the south end of the Dead Sea, but when that dried up, Israeli archaeologists made a detailed search of the area and found no evidence of occupation. The claim has been made that there are formations that seem like buildings and walls just north of Masada, but an Israeli geologist certified that these are purely geological formations.

As they were obviously twin cities it may be that they were on opposite banks of the River Arnon, which flows into the east side of the Dead Sea. The Dead Sea has risen in height since then, so these cities may be buried beneath

◀ *The Destruction of Sodom and Gomorrah painted by John Martin in 1852.*

The Sodom and Gomorrah motif from the Nuremberg Chronicle by Hartmann Schedel, 1493. ▶

silt near the mouth of the Arnon River, but no investigation has been made here so this suggested location is only speculative. And their destruction, spoken of in the Bible, may have been thoroughly complete.

THE OFFERING

Lot lost his wife and his home when the wicked cities were destroyed, but Abraham was about to face a heart-rending choice. Abraham must have been well advanced in years, and his son Isaac by then probably a youth, when God told him to "take now your son, your only son Isaac, whom you love, and go to the land of Moriah, and offer him there as a burnt offering on one of the mountains of which I shall tell you" (Gen. 22:2).

Abraham must have been stunned by this unusual command, not only because the idea of a human sacrifice would seem inconsistent with the God he knew, but because this would result in the death of his only true heir. He had fathered Ishmael by Hagar, and his concubines had borne him sons (Gen. 25:6), but God was now telling him to sacrifice the only son God recognized as his heir.

But Abraham recognized God's authority as supreme and concluded that God would restore Isaac to life. "By faith Abraham, when he was tested, offered up Isaac . . . concluding that God was able to raise him up, even from the dead" (Heb. 11:17–19).

Abraham was residing at Beersheba at the time (Gen. 21:34), and Mount Moriah was 50 miles (80 km) to the northeast. They journeyed for two full days, which must have seemed more like two eternities of anguish for the distressed father. On the third day, Abraham saw the hill that had been shown him in a vision. He must have then been on the Mount of Olives where he left his two assistants and walked the remaining distance, taking only Isaac and the wood he had brought with him. It was then that Isaac asked the question Abraham had been dreading. "Look, the fire and the wood, but where is the lamb for a burnt offering?" (Gen. 22:7). Abraham replied in words that had a deeper significance than he realized. "My son, God will provide for Himself the lamb for a burnt offering" (Gen. 22:8).

When the altar had been built, Abraham broke the news about the sacrifice of his son. Isaac was probably old

◀ *On the cliffs on the western side of the Dead Sea is a prominent pillar that has been called "Lot's wife," but it is simply rock salt and has nothing to do with the true account.*

"Ram in the Thicket" at the British Museum. ▼

A RAM IN THE THICKET

Sir Leonard Woolley found an interesting object in Ur — an animal standing on its hind legs with its front legs resting on a bush. This object is now in the British Museum. Enthusiastic believers seized on it as a memorial to the incident of the ram caught in a thicket as described in the Bible, but actually the animal is a goat and has nothing to do with the story of Abraham.

enough to have escaped the dreadful ordeal, but Abraham had "commanded his household after him, that they keep the way of the Lord" (Gen. 18:19), and Isaac submitted to his terrible fate. "And Abraham stretched out his hand and took the knife to slay his son" (Gen. 22:10). At the last dramatic moment the angel of the Lord intervened, and God did provide an animal for the sacrifice — a ram caught in a thicket (Gen. 22:13).

The drama was ended and Abraham and his son returned to the waiting servants. The patriarch had learned a lesson he would never forget. Not just a lesson in obedience and divine intervention, but about what salvation really depends on — not on an animal or human sacrifice but on the lamb that God Himself would provide. He learned a vivid lesson in what it would mean for God to offer His Son as a sacrifice for a lost world. Abraham "received him in a figurative sense" (Heb. 11:19).

WATER RIGHTS

Water is a vital necessity for life. In the land of Canaan it was often hard to come by. It rains in winter from November to May but then there is not a drop until the next winter, so for the summer months it had to be obtained from wells, springs, or cisterns that had been filled during the wet season. Abraham dug such a well at Beersheba, but some Philistines had come and appropriated the well for their own use.

Sometime later the Philistine king Abimelech came to visit Abraham, and the latter complained about the well his people had seized. Abimelech disclaimed any knowledge of the incident and he and Abraham made a covenant under oath to respect each other's rights. So Abraham "called that place Beersheba, because the two of them swore an oath there" (Gen. 21:31). Beersheba literally means "well of oath."

In the south of Israel is a large Jewish city called Beersheba and it has an old well, but not nearly old enough to have been dug by Abraham. Two and one-half miles (4 km) north of this city is a tell called Tell es-Seba, which some archaeologists suggest was the original Beersheba, and it has a well that was cut down through 130 feet (40 m) of solid rock, but this also was of more recent origin. In any

▲ *View at the excavations of Tel Be'er Sheva, near modern Beersheba.*

▲ *Exterior of the Hebron Mosque, traditional burial place of Abraham and his family.*

case, Abraham was not likely to have dug his well on top of a hill. We would conclude that the site of Abraham's Beersheba well has been lost.

RESTING PLACES

Abraham was in Hebron when his wife Sarah died. From the sons of Heth (Hittites) he purchased a field in which was a cave. Critics have scoffed at Abraham's offer to give Ephron the Hittite "money" for the cave (Gen. 23:8–13). Coins were not minted until about 600 B.C., but the Hebrew word *keseph* used here simply means "silver" and is so translated in verse 16 where it was "weighed out."

Abraham and other members of his family were also buried there. Today a large building stands over a cave in Hebron. Above the cave are false tombs named for Abraham, Sarah, Isaac, Jacob, Rebekah, and Leah. The entrance to the cave is through a small opening on the floor of the building, but it is regarded as so sacred by both Jews and Muslims that no one is allowed into the cave to see what is there.

Whether this is where Abraham and his family were actually buried cannot be verified. The foundation stones of the building are Herodian and date to before the beginning of the Christian era. The stones in the walls are from the 14th century A.D. The Crusaders used it as a church, and in the following Muslim era it was converted into a mosque.

THE WELL OF DISPUTE

The well at Beersheba continued to be a point of dispute between Abraham, Isaac, and the Philistines, but no further incidents are recorded as happening there, though Beersheba was recognized as marking the southern border of the nation of Israel. There are repeated references to the expression "from Dan to Beersheba."

▲ *Interior of the Hebron Mosque.*

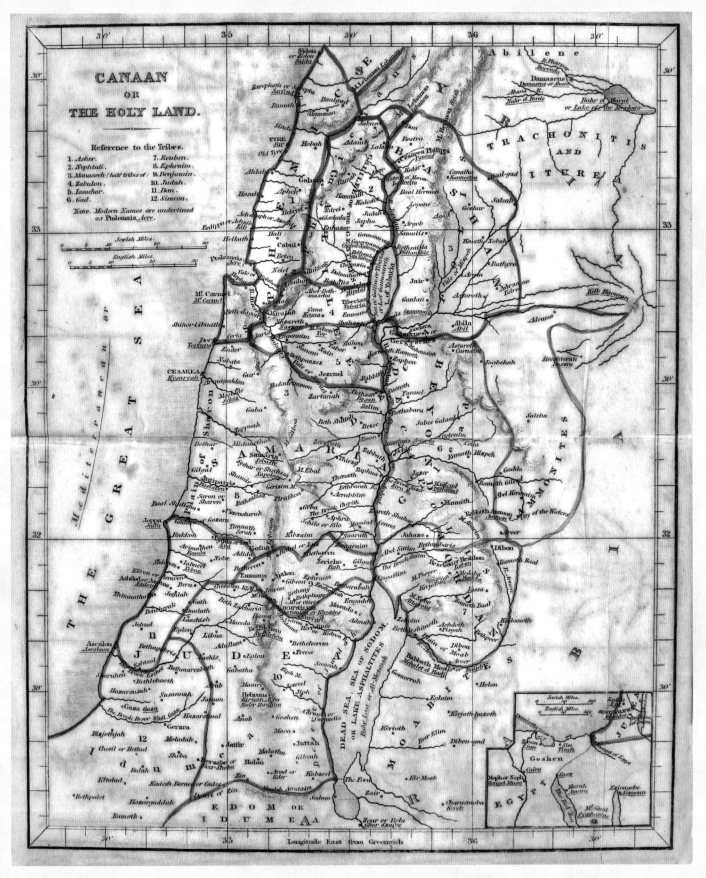

▲ *Vintage map (1836) of the twelve tribes of Israel.*

ANCIENT MARRIAGE CUSTOMS

A Bride in Haran ▲

Home in Canaan

Chapter 4

ISAAC AND REBEKAH

Abraham sent his servant to his family town in Haran to negotiate a bride for his son Isaac. An interesting parallel can be seen in the arrangements for the marriage of the daughters of Zimri-lin of Mari in Western Syria. The servant chose Rebekah who returned with him and married Isaac. To them were born the twins Esau and Jacob. Rebekah induced Jacob to deceive Isaac into cheating Esau, the older of the two, out of the birthright.

GENESIS

IN BIBLE TIMES, MARRIAGES WERE ARRANGED BY PARENTS, as they still are in most Eastern countries today. This had the advantage of cool assessment rather than the impetuous infatuation that often characterizes many modern Western marriages. It has the disadvantage that material gain to the families involved can often determine the results. This was not always in the interests of the prospective bridal pair.

How such negotiations were conducted is revealed in two ancient documents, and Jack M. Sasson discusses the subject in an article in *The Journal of Near Eastern Studies.*[1] The first case is that of the daughters of Zimri Lin, king of Mari in Mesopotamia, and the other story is of the marriage arrangements for Isaac, the son of Abraham, as recorded in Genesis 24, where a whole chapter of 66 verses is devoted to the incident.

Mari, now known as Tell Hariri, was an important city on the west bank of the Euphrates River near the Syria-Iraq border. French archaeologists under Professor Andre Parrot excavated there between 1933 and 1938, and again from 1951 to 1954. They made some spectacular discoveries.

From the archaeological evidence uncovered they determined that Mari had been occupied from the beginning of the Early Bronze Period until it was conquered and destroyed by Sargon of Akkad in the 19th century B.C. A subsequent king, Naram-sin, built a temple to the fertility goddess Ishtar and installed two of his daughters as high priestesses. He also built an enormous palace that ultimately covered six acres and consisted of no less than 260 rooms.

The last great king of Mari was Zimri-lin and from his palace were excavated thousands of cuneiform tablets that provided historians with invaluable information about the history and times of ancient Mari. In the 33rd year of his reign, Hammurabi of Babylon conquered Mari, and when it rebelled against him two years later he systematically pillaged and burned the palace, effectively burying the precious tablets, to be found later by the French archaeologists.

It is from these tablets that Jack Sasson recovered the information about the marriages of Zimri-lin's daughters to kings ruling over his vassal states. But the record of the betrothal of Zimri-lin himself to Princess Siptu in the 18th century B.C. is the most informative. He negotiated for the daughter of Yaram-lin, king of Yamhad, of which Halab, now Aleppo, was the capital. This happened soon after Zimri-lin assumed the throne of Mari.

Zimri-lin was not young at the time and undoubtedly already had numerous wives, so the objectives of the proposed marriage were political. The king entrusted negotiations to two of his courtiers, his chief musician and his diviner. His diviner, Asqudum by name, sent most of the letters to Zimri-lin, and from these letters we glean most of the information. Sasson is particularly intrigued by Asqudum's report that he "draped veils over the young woman."[2]

Expensive gifts were needed to procure the approval of the prospective bride's father. The negotiator started with 20 gold vessels, which Zimri-lin should send, but then added "necklaces, disks, vessels of precious metals, textiles and garments, over a

▼ *Zeugitana, Carthage. Shekel, Circa 310–290 B.C. Wreathed head of Tanit (left). Horse standing right on double ground line (right).*

1.   Jack M. Sasson, "The Servant's Tale: How Rebekah Found a Spouse," *Journal of Near Eastern Studies*, vol. 65, no. 4 (October 2006), p. 241–265.
2.   Ibid., p. 245.

▲ *Shiloh Cistern, a receptacle for storing rainwater.*

▲ *Euphrates River at Ataturk Dam, Anatolia, Turkey.*

hundred cattle, and a thousand sheep."[3]

Of course this was just the starting price. Easterners know how to drive a bargain and negotiations began in earnest. Subsequently added to the list for Yaram-lin were "1 gold ring weighing six shekels (50 grams) . . . 200 sheep. . . . For Galeru (his wife) 1 finely woven fabric, 2 gold clasps weighing 2 shekels, 2 gold clasps weighing 1 shekel, and 20 sheep. For the daughter Siptu, 1 Marad fabric, 2 gold clasps weighing 2 shekels."[4]

Yaram-lin seemed to be satisfied with this offer and Asqudum was able to report that the deal had been struck, though apparently Yaram-lin made some anxious inquiries about where his daughter would be housed. He did not want her to lose her identity in the harem with all the other wives.

From other correspondence it can be learned that Princess Siptu turned up with a retinue of attendants including her wet nurse, a girlhood playmate, and a courier to convey messages back home. It all took time and diplomacy.

A BRIDE FOR ISAAC

Sasson then makes comparisons with the betrothal of Isaac and Rebekah. Abraham was getting on in years and Isaac was by now 40 years old, patiently waiting for his father to start negotiations. Abraham was insistent that his son not marry a Canaanite and commissioned his trusted elder servant to go to his homeland and find a suitable wife from among his kindred in Haran.

This servant was probably the Eliezer mentioned in Genesis 15:2, who set out with ten camels and a wealth of presents for the intended bride and her family (Gen. 24:10). Critics have seized on this text as evidence that the incident is not historical. Bible chronology places Abraham in the 19th century B.C., but they point out that camels were not domesticated until the Iron Age, 1200 B.C. But even if

3.   Ibid., p. 245.
4.   Ibid., p. 246.

there is no historical record of domesticated camels before the Iron Age, that does not prove they did not exist before then. It simply means that archaeologists have not found any evidence that they existed before the Iron Age.

Undoubtedly Eliezer would have been accompanied by a large retinue of servants and guards. Reference is made to "the men who were with him" (Gen. 24:32). Eliezer was a man of strong faith. On arrival at the well of Haran he "made his camels kneel down outside the city by a well of water at evening time, the time when women go out to draw water" (Gen. 24:11).

Then he asked God to indicate which of the women would be a suitable choice for his master's son. He said, "Let it be that the young woman to whom I say, 'Please let down your pitcher that I may drink,' and she says, 'Drink, and I will also give your camels a drink' — let her be the one whom You have appointed for Your servant Isaac" (Gen. 24:14).

Now that was asking for something big. Eliezer had ten camels and Sasson points out that one camel can gulp down more than 25 gallons (100 L) in one session. That would require the maiden to fill her jar at least six times, and for ten camels, that would take about two hours' hard work.

But no sooner had he finished his prayer than a good-looking virgin appeared. Eliezer wasted no time. He ran to meet her and asked for a drink. Water was the gift of life and no Easterner would refuse such a request, but then came the crucial test and Eliezer did not even have to make the request. Rebekah volunteered to draw water for all his camels.

That convinced Eliezer. He did not even wait to find out who she was and promptly produced "a golden nose ring weighing half a shekel, and two bracelets for her wrists weighing ten shekels of gold" (Gen. 24:22), and attached the nose ring to her nostril and put the bracelets on her wrists. He then asked her whose daughter she was and was delighted to learn that she was a relative of Abraham.

▲ *Rebecca and Eliezer by Bartolomé Esteban Murillo, 17th century.*

Apparently her father was incompetent and her elder brother Laban took control of the negotiations.

NUPTIAL NEGOTIATIONS

All of these arrangements were quite customary for Bible times. Sasson notes the similarity in language to God's metaphorical gifts to Jerusalem, his spiritual bride. "I adorned you with ornaments, put bracelets on your wrists, and a chain on your neck. And I put a jewel in your nose, earrings in your ears, and a beautiful crown on your head" (Ezek. 16:11–12).

Eliezer told Laban how Abraham had commissioned him to find a wife for Isaac and asked that Rebekah be allowed to return with him and marry Isaac. To this Laban agreed, and then followed the bridal gifts. He brought out "jewelry of silver, jewelry of gold, and clothing, and gave them to Rebekah. He also gave precious things to her brother and to her mother" (Gen. 24:53). Sasson notes the similarity to the record of Yaram-sin's exchange of marriage gifts. "Attention is given Rebekah who, as did Siptu, receives

precious ornaments and clothing."[5]

Strange that there was nothing for Bethuel, her father. Presumably he was well advanced in years and left everything to his son to negotiate, though there is no mention of any bargaining. Abraham was a generous man and apparently his lavish gifts left nothing to be desired.

RETURNING TO ISAAC

There was, however, one more hurdle to overcome. Laban wanted the bridal party to leave after ten or more days. That would be customary for such an occasion. A similar request had been made for Siptu. But Eliezer was anxious to be on his way. Laban left it to his sister to decide and Rebekah agreed. The group was soon on its way, bearing her family's blessing to be "the mother of thousands of ten thousands" (Gen. 24:60).

It took a long time for that blessing to come to pass. Rebekah was infertile and bore no children for 20 years, and even then it was only the result of divine intervention.

---

5   Ibid., p. 262.

▲ *Cave of the Patriarchs from the south, Israel, Hebron, traditionally thought to be the burial place of three couples: (1) Abraham and Sarah; (2) Isaac and Rebekah; (3) Jacob and Leah.*

Then she had twins, Esau and Jacob, whose Edomite and Israelite children have produced millions of descendants.

The meeting of Isaac and Rebekah is described in language that is greatly intriguing: "Then Rebekah lifted her eyes, and when she saw Isaac she dismounted from her camel; for she had said to the servant, 'Who is this man walking in the field to meet us?' And the servant said, 'It is my master.' So she took a veil and covered herself" (Gen. 24:64–65).

Sasson notes that the Hebrew word for "dismount" is better translated "fall." He does not suggest an embarrassing accident but rather dismounting in haste.[6]

This all sounds very logical. It would be improper for the prospective bride to be on a higher plane than her future husband, so she hastily dismounted and in all due modesty veiled her face. But Sasson sees deeper implications. He claims that Hebrew women did not usually veil their faces. He therefore considers Rebekah's act a recognition of her betrothal to Isaac.

It is a beautiful story, but unfortunately it had an unhappy ending. Rebekah turned out to be a scheming wife who persuaded her favorite son Jacob to practice shameful deceit by convincing his blind father that he was the son who was entitled to inherit the family birthright. Rather anticlimactic, but the Bible does not gloss over the truth. If it happened, it is recorded.

▲ *Hebron tombs of Isaac and Rebekah.*

6.   Ibid.

PETRA'S SIGNIFICANCE

Jacob's Deception ▲   ▲ Burial at Hebron

◀ *The sig is the narrow rock gorge that forms the entrance to Petra.*

Chapter 5

JACOB AND ESAU

After twenty years of marriage Rebekah gave birth to twins, Esau and Jacob. The former became the progenitor of the Edomites and Jacob became the progenitor of the Israelites. Rebekah incited Jacob into deceiving Isaac into bestowing the birthright on Jacob, but Esau threatened to kill Jacob and he was obliged to flee to Haran where he married Leah and Rachel and their handmaidens. Between them they bore twelve children who became the progenitors of the twelve tribes of Israel. After twenty years Jacob returned to his home land where he was reconciled to his brother Esau whose descendants the Edomites later occupied Petra.

The sig is the narrow rock gorge that forms the entrance to Petra.

TWENTY YEARS WENT BY BEFORE REBEKAH BORE ANY children, when she gave birth to twin boys (Gen. 25:20–26). The firstborn was Esau, who was born with an uncommon medical condition called hypertrichosis. Prolific hair grows all over the face and body. His skin was also very red so that he was also known as Edom, the Hebrew word for red (Gen. 25:30). His descendants were known as the Edomites who later occupied Petra.

"The first came out red. He was like a hairy garment all over; so they called his name Esau [Hebrew *ESAV*, meaning "hairy"]. Afterward his brother came out, and his hand took hold of Esau's heel; so his name was called Jacob" (Gen. 25:25–26).

The name Jacob (Hebrew *Yaaqob*) was derived from the Hebrew word *Aqab*, meaning "seize," referring to the newborn Jacob catching hold of Esau's heel as the birth took place (Gen. 25:26).

The two boys developed totally different characters and dispositions. Jacob was more spiritually minded and longed to inherit the birthright that would one day make him the priest of the house. He was his mother's favorite, but Esau loved to hunt and he was Isaac's favorite.

As Isaac advanced in years his eyesight failed him, and he felt it was time to pronounce the customary blessing on the son who should be heir to his possessions. Such a blessing would also confer on this son the family priesthood. He summoned Esau and proposed that he hunt some wild game and make a banquet befitting such an occasion. Esau took his bow and arrows and departed (Gen. 27:1–5).

However, Rebekah had been eavesdropping on this conversation, and she wanted her favorite son Jacob to inherit the birthright. She told him to hastily kill two kids of the goats and she would prepare a banquet for Isaac. Then Jacob would receive the blessing (Gen. 27:5–10).

Jacob mildly protested, but Rebekah insisted and prepared the meat dish. She had Jacob wear Esau's clothes and covered his hands with goat's hair to deceive Isaac into thinking it was Esau. Isaac was apprehensive. He recognized the voice of Jacob and insisted on feeling his hands but was reassured by the hairy feel and proceeded to pronounce the blessing (Gen. 27:11–29).

No sooner was the ceremony completed than Esau arrived with his venison. Isaac was distressed that he had been deceived and Esau was furious at being deprived of the birthright. Isaac pronounced a blessing on Esau, but Esau vowed to kill his brother as soon as his father died (Gen. 27:30–41). Actually, Isaac lived another 43 years.

JACOB FLEES

In the meantime, Rebekah advised Jacob to leave home and go to live with her family in Haran. She feared the wrath of Esau against Jacob. So Jacob set out, stopping at Luz on the way. By this time he was not only feeling apprehensive about the dangers he would meet on his long journey, but he was no doubt feeling guilty for so shamelessly deceiving his father. He lay down to sleep with only a stone for a pillow.

▼ *Isaac with Esau and Jacob by Ghiberti. Detail of the panel on the doors ("Gates of Paradise") of the Duomo Baptistry, Florence, Italy.*

▲ *The Church at Petra is just one of the magnificent structures in this region connected to the Byzantine empire.*

▲ *Jacob's Well Church at Samaria. Jacob returned to Shechem, he camped "before" the city and bought the land. Biblical scholars contend that plot of land is the same one upon which Jacob's Well was constructed.*

That night he had a dream in which he saw a ladder bridging the gulf between heaven and earth. The word used here for ladder is *sullam*, the same word that is used for the steps that lead up to the shrine on top of the ziggurat at Ur, but whereas those steps ascended little more than 160 feet (50 m), these steps reached right up into heaven, God's dwelling place.

Jacob realized that he had erred, but he was encouraged to know he was not forsaken by God. There were still steps up to heaven. He called the name of the place Bethel, meaning "House of God." Jesus referred to this incident when He said to Nathaniel, "Hereafter you shall see heaven open, and the angels of God ascending and descending upon the Son of Man" (John 1:51). Jesus Christ, by His death on the Cross, spanned the gulf between God and a guilty world.

JACOB DECEIVED

In Haran, Jacob stayed with his uncle Laban and fell in love with Laban's daughter Rachel. The crafty Laban required Jacob to work for him for seven years for his daughter's hand in marriage, and then on the marriage night he substituted his other daughter, Leah. In Eastern culture Leah's face would have been veiled, making the deceit practicable. Jacob had deceived his brother. Now it was his turn to be deceived.

When Jacob protested to Laban the next morning, Laban then offered him Rachel for a further seven years' work. Because of fertility problems, Jacob also married the handmaids of his two wives. Between them all he finished up with 12 sons, who became the progenitors of the 12 tribes of Israel.

When Jacob's 14 years of servitude had been fulfilled, Jacob proposed to Laban that he return to his father's land. But Laban knew when he had a good thing and persuaded Jacob to stay on the understanding that Jacob would look after his flocks but that all the speckled or spotted sheep and goats would belong to Jacob.

FLOURISHING FLOCKS

Probably accepting a local belief, Jacob assumed that the color of lambs and kids that were born depended on what the sheep and goats were looking at when they mated, so "the rods which he had peeled, he set before the flocks in the gutters, in the watering troughs where the flocks came to drink, so that they should conceive when they came to drink" (Gen. 30:38).

It seemed to work very well. The next verse says, "So the flocks conceived before the rods, and the flocks brought forth streaked, speckled, and spotted."

Critics were quick to seize on this record and scoff that abnormalities such as this were dependent on genetics, not what the rams were looking at when they mated. But while it is true that at that time Jacob thought that was the secret of reproduction, the angel taught him otherwise. Jacob

THE BRIDAL VEIL

Was Laban's deceit of Jacob common practice of the time? There were no civil laws about marriage celebrations, and often it was not until the ceremonies were all finished that the groom was permitted to lift his bride's veil and get his first look at her face.

FAMILY DUTY AND HONOR

The eldest son was regarded as the family priest at this time in Israel. He would offer sacrifices for the family and conduct all of the religious ceremonies throughout the seasons. It was this prestige that was so vital, and Esau despised Jacob taking this from him by his deception.

said, "The angel of God spoke to me in a dream saying . . . all the rams which leap on the flocks are streaked, speckled, and gray-spotted" (Gen. 31:11–12). Jacob finished up with a huge flock.

After 20 years in Haran, Jacob finally decided to return to his homeland. When he reached Mahanaim he sent a message to Esau announcing his return, and lest Esau should think that he would now claim the family possessions, he told him that he now possessed all the flocks and herds he needed. His servants returned with the disquieting news that Esau was on his way with 400 men, obviously bent on revenge.

A PRAYER IN THE NIGHT

That night by the River Jabbok, Jacob spent an anxious night praying. This was a matter of life and death for Jacob and his family, and his prayers were answered. A mysterious assailant touched him and said, "Your name shall no longer be called Jacob, but Israel; for you have struggled with God and with men, and have prevailed" (Gen. 32:28). Jacob meant "heel-catcher," Israel meant "Prince with God," or "God is upright," which would be a big contrast to Jacob the heel catcher, or deceiver.

As Jacob approached Esau, Jacob "bowed himself to the ground seven times, until he came near to his brother" (Gen. 33:3). This was consistent with the customs of the day of one who acknowledges the superiority of one in authority. In the Amarna letters, correspondence on clay tablets found at Amarna in Egypt, there are frequent such

▲ The Petra Garden Tomb, which connects to a steep rock wall and immense cistern used by the Nabataeans.

▲ River Jabbok, where Jacob spent the night praying.

◄ A tomb on the road between Jerusalem and Bethlehem was considered to be Rachel's burial place

references. Abdi-Heba, king of Jerusalem, wrote to the king of Egypt, saying, "I fall at the feet of the king my lord 7 times and 7 times."[1] And Suwadata wrote to the king saying, "I fall at the feet of my lord 7 times and 7 times, both on the stomach and on the back."[2]

A reconciliation ensued, with Esau returning to his home in Seir and Jacob proceeding to Succoth and Shechem. The Genesis record says that Jacob purchased land at Shechem but makes no reference to him digging a well there. Yet when Jesus spoke to the woman of Samaria and offered her living water she asked him, "Are you greater than our father Jacob, who gave us the well, and drank from it himself, as well as his sons and his livestock?" (John 4:12).

Jacob's Well is one of the few authentic sites in Israel. It is now sheltered under a church, and as the woman said, "the well is deep" (John 4:11). Its depth is 105 feet (32 m). That is a long way to dig down, and how did they know they were going to strike water there?

---

1.   Amarna Letter EA288.
2.   Amarna Letter EA281.

THE POWER OF THE BLESSING

Why couldn't Isaac simply change his mind and bless Esau once the deceit was revealed? The pronounced blessing was irrevocable. All Isaac could do was pronounce an inferior blessing on Esau.

SHECHEM TO BETHEL

It was at Shechem that Jacob's daughter disgraced herself by going out to see the daughters of the land and finishing up by being raped by the prince of Shechem. Jacob's sons Simeon and Levi took their revenge by slaughtering all the males in Shechem and plundering all their possessions. Jacob feared that the surrounding Canaanites and Perizzites would likewise seek revenge. No doubt he prayed for divine

▲ *Named from the central figure, a Roman soldier carved in stone, Soldier Tomb is connected to a beautiful colonnaded courtyard.*

▲ *Petra has over 800 tombs carved in stone.*

protection and God advised him to move on to Bethel (Gen. 35:1).

Apparently Jacob wanted to put as much distance as possible between his tribe and the people of Shechem, so he continued his journey south on the way to Ephrath, later known as Bethlehem. On the way, Jacob's favorite wife, Rachel, died in giving birth to Benjamin, the last of Jacob's sons. She was buried "on the way to Ephrath (that is Bethlehem)" (Gen. 35:19).

In the Byzantine period, a tomb on the road between Jerusalem and Bethlehem was considered to be Rachel's burial place, and a small domed building marked the site. It has more recently been built over by a modern structure for security for the many Jews who go there to mourn. It is regarded as the third most sacred site in Israel for Jewish pilgrims. Actually, it is not likely to be the site of Rachel's tomb because 1 Samuel 10:2 says it was in the territory of Benjamin, and that was north of Jerusalem, not south where the traditional tomb is.

DESCENDANTS OF ESAU

Esau returned to the land he had occupied, which was called Seir. His

descendents occupied Sela, meaning "rock" (Isa. 16:1). In the Greek period it was known as Petra, also meaning "rock."

The Edomites were always hostile to Israel, and when the Babylonians besieged Jerusalem the Edomites allied with the Babylonians and urged them, "Raze it, raze it, to its very foundation" (Ps. 137:7). For this show of hostility God decreed that the Edomites would themselves be wiped out.

The prophet Obadiah addressed them with the words, "You who dwell in the clefts of the rock. . . . For violence against your brother Jacob, shame shall cover you, and you shall be cut off forever" (Obad. 1:3–10). Jeremiah added, "No one shall remain there" (Jer. 49:18). The main entrance to Petra is through a narrow ravine almost a mile (1.5 km) long. Obadiah appropriately calls it "clefts of the rock."

In the fourth century B.C., the Nabateans occupied Petra and squeezed the Edomites out. They migrated to southern Israel and were later converted to Judaism. Herod the Great was an Edomite, and it was he who killed all the babies in Bethlehem soon after Christ was born.

This Tree shews that when Jacob arrived in Egypt, his whole family, including Joseph & his two children amounted to 70 persons. Jacob himself, and sixty four sons and grandsons, one daughter Dinah, and one granddaughter Sarah. These 67 persons, added to Joseph and his two sons who were already in Egypt, make up the numbers exactly 70.

JACOB
Genesis. XXX. XLVI.

The two sons of Judah, Er, and Onan, who died in Canaan Jacob's wives, their handmaidens, and his son's wives, or other connections are not taken into the number 70. here Gen. XLVI. but in Acts VII. 14.

▲ *Jacob family tree from Leonard's Chronological Chart of History (c. 1860).*

PETRA'S PROSPERITY

In the meantime, Petra became a prosperous and spectacular city with tombs and temples carved out of the colorful cliffs. In A.D. 106 the Romans occupied Petra and it became even more prosperous. When Christianity became the state religion of the Roman Empire, an impressive church and monastery, presided over by a bishop, was built in Petra, but its doom, though long delayed, was at last realized. Under Islam, Petra lost its importance. The Crusaders built a small castle there but when they left Petra became unoccupied. The city was deserted and lapsed into silence until it was discovered by John Burkhardt in 1812.

Isaac lived to the ripe old age of 180 years (Gen. 35:28). Once more the twin brothers came together. They buried their father in the family tomb at Hebron.

▼ *The magnificence of the ruins of Petra, once home to nearly 30,000 people.*

SLAVERY IN EGYPT

Home in Dothan ▲   ▲ Fleeing to Midian

Chapter 6

JOSEPH TO MOSES

Joseph was Jacob's favorite son to whom he gave a coat of many colors. When Joseph visited his brothers at Dothan they sold him to some traders who took him to Egypt where he was sold as a slave.

While there Joseph interpreted the dreams of Pharaoh's butler and baker. Two years later Joseph correctly interpreted Pharaoh's dream to mean there would be seven years plenty followed by seven years famine. Pharaoh appointed Joseph to prepare the country for the coming famine. The famine was felt in Canaan and Joseph's brothers came to Egypt to buy food. Joseph arranged for his whole family to take up residence in Egypt. They multiplied to some two million souls who departed in the Exodus under Moses.

GENESIS

JACOB'S FAVORITE SON WAS JOSEPH, TO WHOM HE GAVE a coat of many colors. By the reduced chronology for the dynasties of Egypt advocated by some scholars this incident would have occurred during Dynasty 12. From this period there are pictures of high-class people dressed in very colorful clothes.

However, this favoritism shown to Joseph aroused the jealousy of his older brothers. To make matters worse, Joseph had two dreams predicting that his brothers would one day bow down to him, and he was indiscreet enough to tell his brothers what he had dreamed.

Fodder must have been scarce at Hebron, because the brothers went to Shechem, 46 miles (75 km) north of Hebron, to find pasture. They were away so long that Jacob, who knew where they had gone, sent Joseph to find them and inquire about their welfare. Joseph searched for them at Shechem without success, but he met a man who knew of their activities. He told him that the brothers had announced their intention of going to Dothan, which was 15 miles (25 km) farther north.

A MURDER PLOT

As with most cities in the Old Testament era, Dothan was built on a hill, but in the area are fertile plains where the brothers could have found pasture. They saw Joseph coming and their hostility was aroused at the sight of his coat of many colors. "Look," they said, "this dreamer is coming! Come therefore, let us now kill him and cast him into some pit; and we shall say, 'Some wild beast has devoured him.' We shall see what will become of his dreams!" (Gen. 37:19–20.)

Reuben was rather apprehensive about this proposal. As the eldest of the brothers he felt a sense of responsibility and shrank from the idea of killing Joseph, so he suggested casting him into a pit. He intended to later rescue him.

On Joseph's arrival the ten brothers grabbed him, stripped him of his hated colored coat, and dropped him into a nearby cistern used for preserving water. The drought in the land must have been rather severe because there was no water in the cistern. The brothers then settled down to enjoy a meal, gratified that they had at last gotten their revenge on their hated younger brother.

SLAVERY IN EGYPT

While they were enjoying their repast, a group of Midianite traders on their camels passed by on their way to Egypt. Judah thought it a good opportunity to make a quick shekel and suggested they sell Joseph as a slave to the passing traders. They hauled Joseph out of the cistern and sold him for 20 shekels of silver.

Reuben was distraught when he returned to find what his brothers had done, but it was too late to change anything, so they killed a kid of the goats and dipped Joseph's tunic in the blood. On their return to Hebron they showed Jacob the tunic. The old father was distraught at the thought that his beloved son had been killed by a wild beast, and went into a long period of mourning.

The Midianite traders took Joseph to Egypt and sold him to Potiphar, a high-ranking officer of Pharaoh. Joseph decided that if he had to be a slave he might as well be a good one, and performed his duties conscientiously. His diligence paid off. Potiphar recognized that he prospered because of Joseph's loyalty to his God, and he promoted

▼ *Carved stone head of Senusret III, considered the most powerful Egyptian ruler of the 12th Dynasty.*

▲ *The exterior of the Beni Hassan tomb near modern-day Minya.* ▲ *Entryway to the Beni Hassan tomb.* ▲ *Looking west from the region of Dothan.*

Joseph to be overseer of his household. But tragedy for Joseph was lurking in the background.

ENSLAVED AND IMPRISONED

Genesis 37:36 says that Potiphar was "an officer of Pharaoh." The word used here for officer is *SERIYS*, which can mean "eunuch." It is so translated in the New English Bible. It was not uncommon for high-ranking eunuchs to be married, which may have left some of their wives rather frustrated, besides which "Joseph was handsome in form and appearance" (Gen. 39:6). The result was that she "cast longing eyes on Joseph, and she said, 'Lie with me' " (Gen. 39:7).

Joseph determined to be loyal to his God and politely refused, but she was not about to give up. "She spoke to Joseph day by day" (verse 10). Joseph steadfastly declined and took pains to avoid her company, but one day while in the house doing his business, there happened to be no one else in the house, and she grabbed his garment and urged him to lie with her. Egypt can be very hot, and men wore only one loose garment. When Joseph tried to flee she held on to his garment and he had to flee naked.

Potiphar's wife did not take kindly to being spurned by a slave, and on her husband's return she triumphantly displayed Joseph's garment, which she blatantly claimed Joseph had left behind when he had tried to rape her. If Potiphar had fully believed his wife's accusations he would have immediately put Joseph to death. Instead he confined him to prison. Joseph was a model prisoner, and the keeper of the prison soon recognized it and placed Joseph in charge of all the other prisoners.

Sometime later, Pharaoh committed his chief butler and his chief baker to prison, and they were put under Joseph's supervision. While there they each had a dream that Joseph interpreted. The butler's dream meant that he would be restored to his former position, but the baker would lose his head. It happened as Joseph had predicted, but before the butler left the prison Joseph implored him to intercede on his behalf to get him out of the prison.

THE DREAM

The butler soon forgot his obligation to Joseph and two long years went by, but then Pharaoh had a dream that his wise men could not interpret. It was then that the butler remembered Joseph and told Pharaoh of this young Hebrew who could interpret dreams. Pharaoh summoned him from prison.

There seems to be a rather inconsequential detail mentioned here in the Bible record. It says that Joseph "shaved" (Gen. 41:14). But actually it is significant. Joseph, a Hebrew, would have allowed his beard to grow, but most Egyptians were clean-shaven and it would not have been appropriate for Joseph to appear before Pharaoh unshaven.

Joseph interpreted Pharaoh's dreams to mean that there would be seven years of plenty in the land of Egypt, to be followed by seven years of famine, and advised Pharaoh to appoint officers to supervise the collection of grain in preparation for the expected years of famine. Pharaoh accepted Joseph's advice and even appointed Joseph to be vizier over the land of Egypt to supervise the project.

WHICH PHARAOH?

By the Bible chronology, Joseph's appointment would have been in the year 1669 B.C., and by the traditional Egyptian chronology this would have been during the Hyksos era. But there is no supporting archaeological evidence for the existence of Joseph or for a long famine during this period. However, by the reduced chronology for the dynasties of Egypt there is abundant evidence for both.

Sesostris I would have been the 12th Dynasty pharaoh who appointed Joseph to this post. The Bible says that

◄ Associated with abundance, this relief of Hapi depicts the lotus and the papyrus.

Pharaoh had Joseph "ride in the second chariot which he had; and they cried out before him, 'Bow the knee!' " (Gen. 41:43). It was abnormal for someone who was not of the royal family to be shown such respect, but Sesostris did have such a highly respected vizier. He was known by the Egyptian name of Mentuhotep and civilians were obliged to bow down before him.

FAMINE AND FAMILY

At this time an Egyptian provincial governor by the name of Ameni left a record on his tomb wall at Beni Hassan of how he stored quantities of grain for the time of famine. The inscription reads, "No one was unhappy in my days, not even in the years of famine, for I had tilled all the fields of the Nome of Mah, up to its southern and northern frontiers. Thus I prolonged the life of its inhabitants and preserved the food which it produced."[1]

The famine was severe and its effects were felt in the land of Canaan, and Joseph's brothers were obliged to come to Egypt to plead for food. It had been 22 years since they had sold Joseph into slavery, and they did not recognize him when they were ushered into his august presence. When he finally disclosed his identity they were petrified with fear that he would take revenge, but the noble Joseph assured them that no harm would befall them, and that it was not they who had sent him to Egypt but God (Gen. 45:8). He then arranged for his whole family to come to Egypt and settle in the land of Goshen in the northeast delta.

JACOB MUMMIFIED

Seventeen years later Jacob died and Joseph commanded the embalmers to embalm his father. "Forty days were required for him, for such are the days required for those who are embalmed; and the Egyptians mourned for him seventy days" (Gen. 50:3). This is consistent with the known process of mummification in Egypt. The Greek traveler Herodotus wrote, "The body is placed in natron, covered over entirely for seventy days — never longer. When this period, which must not be exceeded, is over, the body is washed and then wrapped from head to foot in linen, cut into strips and smeared with gum which is commonly used by the Egyptians instead of glue."[2]

1.   Heinrich Brugsch Bey, *Egypt Under the Pharaohs* (London: J. Murray; New York: Scriber, 1891), p. 158.

2.   Herodotus, *Herodotus: The Histories*, translated by Walter Blanco, edited by Walter Blanco and Jennifer Tolbert Roberts (New York: Norton, 1992), p. 160.

▲ *Mural on the Beni Hassan tomb near modern day Minya in Egypt depicting nomadic merchants.*

"But the children of Israel were fruitful and increased abundantly, multiplied and grew exceedingly mighty; and the land was filled with them" (Exod. 1:7). Jewish people have always been enterprising businessmen, and it is not surprising that they expanded far beyond the land of Goshen. A picture on the wall of a nobleman by the name of Khnumhotep, whose tomb is in Beni Hassan, depicts foreign traders visiting the province. By the reduced chronology they would have been Israelites, and this would be the first known picture of early Israelites. They wore coats of many colors.

The second to the last king of Dynasty 12 was Sesostris III, a nasty-looking character who is known to have been a tyrant. It would have been he who "set taskmasters over them to afflict them" (Exod. 1:11).

MOSES DISCOVERED

His son was Amenemhet III, who was also a disagreeable looking pharaoh who ruled for 48 years. He had no sons, only two daughters, one of whom seems to have died prematurely. The other daughter, Sobekneferu, had no children. She would have been the daughter of Pharaoh who "came down to bathe at the river" (Exod. 2:5).

It was not that she had no bathroom in the palace. She would have been taking a ceremonial ablution praying to the river god, who was also the fertility god, for a baby to continue the pharaonic line when she saw the baby Moses in a basket and regarded this as an answer to her prayer. She adopted him and intended that he should be the next pharaoh.

FROM FAVORED TO FUGITIVE

But when Moses was 40 years of age he saw an Egyptian mistreating one of the Israelite slaves and killed him. This became known to Pharaoh and Moses was obliged to flee to the land of Midian where he stayed for 40 years. Amenemhet died soon after, and having no son to inherit the throne he was succeeded by his daughter Sobekneferu. She died four years later and the dynasty came to an end, to be succeeded by a quick succession of kings in Dynasty 13.

It was probably during the reign of Neferhotep I that God spoke to Moses and told him to return to Egypt and say to Pharaoh, "Let my people go" (Exod. 5:1). Pharaoh refused this demand and there followed the ten devastating plagues, the last one being the death of all the firstborn in Egypt.

Before the tenth plague God told Moses to command every Israelite household to kill a lamb and "take some of the blood, and put it on the two doorposts and on the lintel of the houses. . . . For I will pass through the land of Egypt on that night, and will strike all the firstborn in the land of Egypt. . . . And when I see the blood, I will pass over you" (Exod. 12:7–13).

Every year the Israelites were to celebrate this Passover ceremony to remind them of this miraculous deliverance from Egypt. The death of the Passover lamb prefigured the death of Christ on the Cross. Paul wrote in 1 Corinthians 5:7, "Christ, our Passover, was sacrificed for us."

When Pharaoh discovered his son was dead he summoned Moses and told him to "rise, go out from among my people, both you and the children of Israel" (Exod. 12:31). The Israelites were ready and they "journeyed from Rameses to Succoth, about six hundred thousand men on foot, besides children" (Exod. 12:37). Counting wives, children, and old people there would have been some two million people who set out for the Promised Land.

ADDING IT UP

Some scholars have questioned this number. They suggest that *ELEPH*, the Hebrew word for "thousand," can also be translated "family." That is true, though there is only one instance in the Hebrew Bible where it is used in that sense. However, in this instance it must be "thousands" because when all the able-bodied men were told to bring a half shekel of silver for the building of the sanctuary, it amounted to 301,775 shekels, representing 603,550 able-bodied men (Exod. 38:35–36). You might be able to make men into families, but you can hardly make shekels into families.

Critics have loudly scoffed that there is no evidence for Israelite slaves in Egypt at this time, and no evidence for an exodus from Egypt.

◄ *Egyptian pharaoh Neferhotep I, who some believe was ruling when God called Moses to free His people.*

▲ *Stone face of pharaoh Neferhotep*

▲ *Kahun beehive*

▲ Closeup of the face of Neferhotep from his tomb

▲ Ruins at the site of the Kahun temple

By the traditional chronology that is undeniable, but there is abundant evidence for Semitic slaves in late Dynasty 12. During Dynasty 13 they suddenly disappeared, and the archaeologists do not know how that could happen. They could if they recognized that these departing slaves were the Israelites in the Exodus.

Well-known Egyptologist Dr. Rosalie David wrote in her book *The Pyramid Builders of Ancient Egypt*:

> It is apparent that the Asiatics were present in the town in some numbers, and this may have reflected the situation elsewhere in Egypt. . . . Their exact homeland in Syria or Palestine cannot be determined. . . . The reason for their presence in Egypt remains unclear.[3]
>
> The scattered documentation gives no clear answer as to how or why the Asiatics came to Egypt in the Middle Kingdom. . . . There is nevertheless firm literary evidence that Asiatic slaves, women and children, were at Gurob, and that some received instruction in workshops.[4]

It is apparent that the completion of the king's pyramid was not the reason why Kahun's inhabitants eventually deserted the town, abandoning their tools and other possessions in the shops and houses.[5]

There are different opinions of how this first period of occupation at Kahun drew to a close. . . . The quantity, range, and type of articles of everyday use which were left behind in the houses may indeed suggest that the departure was sudden and unpremeditated.[6]

It should be obvious that these immigrants from Syria or Palestine were the descendants of Jacob. Their sudden and unpremeditated departure was when they dropped their tools, for which they would have no future use, and left the towns to gather in the land of Goshen ready for their sudden departure in the Exodus.

3. A. Rosalie David, *The Pyramid Builders of Ancient Egypt* (London; Boston: Routledge & K. Paul, 1986), p. 191.
4. Ibid., p. 192.

5. Ibid., p. 195.
6. Ibid., p. 199.

▼ A body that went through the mummification process, involving the use of salts to remove moisture from the corpse.

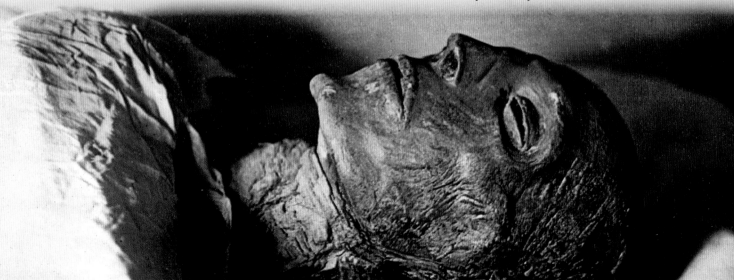

THE SINAI PENINSULA

Freedom from Egypt ▲   The Promised Land

Chapter 7

CROSSING SINAI PENINSULA

After the Israelites had eaten their Passover supper God slew all the first-born in Egypt and Pharaoh gave Israel permission to leave. The only logical place for the crossing of the Red Sea was at Nuveiba where the sea is only a maximum of eight meters deep. Israel then proceeded to Mount Sinai. The traditional mount cannot be the correct site. The Israelites are more likely to have continued straight east across the desert toward Eilat. Jebel Ram is a possible candidate. The Israelites then moved to Kadesh Barnea.

EXODUS

WHEN PHARAOH GAVE THE WAITING ISRAELITES permission to leave Egypt, they were ready. They had eaten their Passover supper and the moment Pharaoh said, "Take your flocks and your herds, as you have said, and be gone" (Exod. 12:32), they started on their journey. From the land of Goshen they would have traveled south to the Red Sea. "God led the people around by way of the wilderness of the Red Sea" (Exod. 13:18).

As the Hebrew words used here are *yam suph*, meaning "Sea of Reeds," some have claimed that it applies to the Great Bitter Lake that is between the Mediterranean Sea and the Red Sea. But *yam suph* undoubtedly applies to what we know as the Red Sea. In fact, it even applies to the Red Sea on the eastern side of the Sinai Peninsula (Num. 14:25, 21:4).

"Now the Lord spoke to Moses, saying: 'Speak to the children of Israel, that they turn and camp before Pi Hahiroth, between Migdol and the sea, opposite Baal Zephon" (Exod. 14:1–2). It all sounds very specific. Unfortunately, none of the place names mentioned on this journey can be positively identified.

FINDING THE CROSSING

By this time Pharaoh had had some second thoughts about losing all his slaves, and he set out in pursuit. "Then Moses stretched out his hand over the sea; and the Lord caused the sea to go back by a strong east wind all that night, and made the sea into dry land" (Exod. 14:21). The Israelites were able to cross to the other side, but when the Egyptians followed them the sea closed in on them and the entire army perished. "The waters returned and covered the chariots, the horsemen, and all the army of Pharaoh that came into the sea after them" (Exod. 14:28).

On one occasion I decided to search for the place where this crossing could have taken place. I hired a rental car and drove from Cairo to the top end of the Red Sea and traveled south. I really do not know what I expected to find in the way of evidence, but I did it anyway.

Six miles (10 km) south at Adabiya I was confronted with a range of mountains

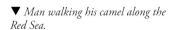
▼ *Man walking his camel along the Red Sea.*

▲ *Camels resting near Mount Sinai, also known as Mount Horeb.*

▲ *Mount Sinai is the place where Moses received the Ten Commandments from God and is considered sacred by the Christian, Jewish, and Muslim religions.*

that dipped down into the sea. I was impressed. If this was the route the Israelites took I could understand their distress. The Red Sea on the left, a mountain blocking their path before them, a dreary desert to the right, and Pharaoh's chariots bearing down on them from the rear. My only question was, how deep was the water here?

When I returned home I was delighted to be able to buy a British Admiralty map of the area. Nothing could be more authentic. I was interested to find that the water north of here was deep and south of here was also deep, but there was a bar about 1,600 feet (half a kilometer) in width from one side to the other, and the maximum depth from the Egyptian shore to the Sinai Peninsula was a maximum of 26 feet (8 m). It was 4.3 miles (7 km) from one side to the other, narrow enough for Israel to cross in one night but wide enough to accommodate Pharaoh's army. It would still take a miracle, but at least it seems plausible that the crossing could have taken place here.

OTHER THEORIES

Since then there have been at least two professional programs on TV claiming that the crossing took place at Nuweiba in the Gulf of Aqaba. They point out that there is a sand bar here and the Israelites could have crossed over it into Arabia. What they do not mention is that, according to my Admiralty map, the minimum depth of this bar is one-half mile (800 m). This would have the Israelites skidding down one side and scrambling up the other. Quite impossible.

There is also the impossibility of Pharaoh's army crossing the 186 miles (300 km) of the Sinai Desert. The Israelites had manna for food and water miraculously provided out of the rock. Pharaoh's army had no such facilities and would have had to take all their food and water with them, and there were no tar-sealed roads across the desert in those days — just a sandy waste.

"In the third month after the children of Israel had gone out of the land of Egypt, on the same day, they came to the Wilderness of Sinai. . . . So Israel camped there before the mountain" (Exod. 19:1–2). Tradition has it that after the Red Sea crossing they turned south and made their way to what is today known as Jebel Musa (Mount of Moses), the second highest mountain in the region. Here God proclaimed to them the Ten Commandments.

LOCATING THE MOUNTAIN

There are some good reasons why this site is quite impossible. In the first place, God said to Moses, "The Lord will come down upon Mount Sinai in the sight of all the people" (Exod. 19:11). There is no way two million people could see Jebel Musa from where they were camped. Jebel Musa is surrounded by rugged mountains, and it takes 45 minutes of stiff climbing from Santa Katarina, the monastery at the foot of the mountains, until Jebel Musa can even be seen. From the crest of this mountain the scenery is awesome, but it is not where the law was proclaimed.

Then Deuteronomy 1:2 says, "It is eleven days' journey from Horeb [Sinai] by way of Mount Seir to Kadesh Barnea." There is no way that two million people with all their flocks and herds could make this 155-mile (250 km) journey in 11 days.

Anyway, it is obviously in the wrong place. When Moses escaped from Pharaoh he "fled from the face of Pharaoh and dwelt in the land of Midian" (Exod. 2:15). Midian was east of the Gulf of Aqaba, not in the south Sinai Peninsula. It was here while he was minding his sheep he "came to Horeb [Sinai], the mountain of God" and saw the burning bush (Exod. 3:1).

Paul also refers to "Mount Sinai in Arabia" (Gal. 4:25). The south Sinai Peninsula is not in Arabia, so we must look elsewhere for this sacred mountain. It is logical to assume that after Israel had crossed the Red Sea the pillar of cloud

▲ *Coastline of the Red Sea in Egypt, known in Arabic as Bahr el Ahmar.*

would have led them directly east toward Arabia.

There are several mountains in this area that could qualify. I think that Jebel Ram where Lawrence of Arabia lodged could be a likely candidate. There is a large area of desert in front of the mount where the Israelites could have pitched their tents, but there could be other candidates for the site.

DESERT JOURNEY LENGTHENED

Wherever Mount Sinai was, after one year the cloud lifted and they proceeded to Kadesh Barnea, which is only 37 miles (60 km) west of the Jordan Valley and 50 miles (80 km) south of Beersheba. It is a clump of hills in the desert with a good water supply, and here Moses sent out 12 representatives of the tribes to spy out the Promised Land.

After 40 days the spies returned with a good report about the land but a pessimistic report of their chances of occupying it. "The people who dwell in the land are strong; the cities are fortified" (Num. 13:28). "The cities are great and fortified up to heaven" (Deut. 1:28). Most of the people, ever ready to find some complaint against Moses, burst into tears and "wept that night" (Num. 14:1). They voted to return to Egypt (Num. 14:4). For this rebellion they were condemned to 40 years of wandering in the wilderness.

Two million people staying in Kadesh Barnea for so long would have left a lot of broken pottery, which archaeologists should be able to find. They have. Dr. Rudolph Cohen, for many years head of the Israeli Antiquities authority, excavated here when Israel was in possession of the Sinai Peninsula following the Six Day War in 1967. He made some interesting discoveries. He was impressed with the large amount of pottery from the Middle Bronze I period he found there and concluded that this was indicative of the Israelites who had stayed there.

He wrote an article for the *Biblical Archaeology Review,* in which he stated:

> One of the most obscure periods in the history of Palestine is the Middle Bronze I period (commonly referred to as MBI) which extended from about 2200 B.C. to about 2000. Who were the MBI people? We really don't know. . . . In fact, these MBI people may be the Israelites whose famous journey from Egypt to Canaan is called the Exodus.[1]
>
> On one thing scholars are agreed. The pottery, the settlements, and other aspects of the material culture of the MBI people that have been uncovered over the last fifty years differ significantly from what went before in the Early Bronze period and from

1. Rudolph Cohen, "The Mysterious MBI People," *Biblical Archaeology Review* (July 1983): p. 16.

▲ *Hatzeva Gate at the entrance to Hatzeva Fortress.*

what followed in the Middle Bronze II period. The Early Bronze Age (c.3150 B.C.–2200 B.C.) was characterized by a flourishing urban civilization. The same was true of the Middle Bronze Age II (c. 2000 B.C.–1550 B.C.). In MBI, however, there was a notable absence of urban settlements.[2]

I have been studying the MBI sites in the Central Negev for almost two decades now. The result of this study can, I believe, elucidate some of the outstanding issues. . . . New aspects of MBI culture, including burial customs and social structure, imply a new ethnic element. Thus, the MBI culture is also intrusive, migrating people who destroyed the existing urban centres must be involved. . . . In my view, the new MBI population came from the south and the Sinai, the route of the Israelites on that journey known as the Exodus. . . . Literally hundreds of MBI sites have been surveyed in the Central Negev.[3]

On the basis of my own excavations and surveys in the Central Negev, however, I believe that the MBI people did not come from the north, or northeast; on the contrary, there is evidence pointing to their origins in the south or southwest.[4]

This migratory drift, as I have reconstructed it, bears a striking similarity to that of the Israelites'

flight from Egypt to the Promised Land, as recorded in the Book of Exodus. The concentration of MBI sites in the relatively fertile district east of Kadesh Barnea recalls the tradition that the Israelites camped near this oasis for 38 of their 40 years of wandering after leaving Egypt (Deuteronomy 1:46).

The establishment of the MBI settlements directly over the ruins of the EBII-EBIII sites in the Central Negev is consistent with the tradition that the Israelites dwelled in the area previously inhabited by their Amalekite foes (Deuteronomy 25:17–19). The northeastward migration of the MBI population into Transjordan has parallels in the biblical recollection that the Israelites remained in Moab before crossing the Jordan River and laying siege to Jericho (Deuteronomy 3:29). In this connection too it is interesting to note that Early Bronze Age Jericho was destroyed by a violent conflagration, and the site was thinly reoccupied by MBI newcomers, who were apparently unaccustomed to urban dwellings. . . . God specifically instructed that these cities should not be rebuilt. Interestingly enough, after the EBIII destruction of Jericho and Ai, both cities lay in ruins for hundreds of years.[5]

The similarity between the course of the MBI migration and the route of the Exodus seem too close

2. Ibid., p. 17.
3. Ibid., p. 19.
4. Ibid., p. 25.

5. Ibid., p. 28.

to be coincidental. The Late Bronze Age (1550–1200 B.C.) — the period usually associated with the Israelites' flight from Egypt — is archaeologically unattested in the Kadesh Barnea area (as elsewhere in the Central Negev, for that matter), but MBI remains abound and seem to provide a concrete background for the traditions of settlement. Whether the Israelites' trek from Egypt actually occurred in this period or was based on a dim memory of an earlier migration and conquest along this route cannot be determined with certainty. But the background of the journey seems clearly to be related to that mysterious archaeological period we so dryly call MBI.[6]

Cohen did not conclude that the dates were wrong but that the Bible date for the occupation of Canaan was wrong, and that the period of the Judges was centuries longer than indicated in the Bible.

ISRAELITE INVADERS?

I first met Rudolph Cohen in 1992. At the time I was involved in excavations at Ein Yael, a few kilometers out of Jerusalem. I happened to pick up a piece of pottery with concentric lines on it and showed it to Gershon Edelstein, the Israeli archaeologist with whom I was excavating. "Look, Gershon," I said, "MBI pottery."

"Yes, Canaanite," he responded.

"Not Canaanite," I replied, "Israelite."

"Yes, I know your views," he said in good humor. "For that matter Rudolph Cohen believes the same." I pricked up my ears. I knew Rudolph Cohen was head of the Israel Antiquities Authority, and that afternoon I visited his office. That was the beginning of a long friendship. In fact, when that first interview was over I said to him, "Rudolph, I bring a group of Australian volunteers here every year, and next year I would like them to work on your excavations." He readily agreed and the following year we worked at Ein Hatzeva, 19 miles (30 km) south of the Dead Sea.

One day while we were at the work site, Egal Israel, supervisor at the dig on the other side of the tell, came to visit us. We had a nice conversation and I concluded by asking him a question: "Egal, Rudolph Cohen believes that the MBI people were the invading Israelites. Do you agree with that?"

"Of course I do," he replied. "All of us down here

believe the same thing."

I said, "The archaeologists up north don't believe that."

"They do not have the experience in the Negev that we have," he replied.

Cohen's conclusions were not accepted by the majority of Israeli archaeologists who cling to a chronology based on synchronisms with Egypt, but as pointed out in *Unwrapping the Pharaohs*, Egyptian chronology is based on a shaky foundation and needs to be reduced by centuries. So should the dates assigned to the corresponding archaeological strata in Israel.

---

6.   Ibid., p. 29.

◄ *View of Mount Sinai from an entryway.*

Journeyings map from Leonard's Chronological Chart of History ▶

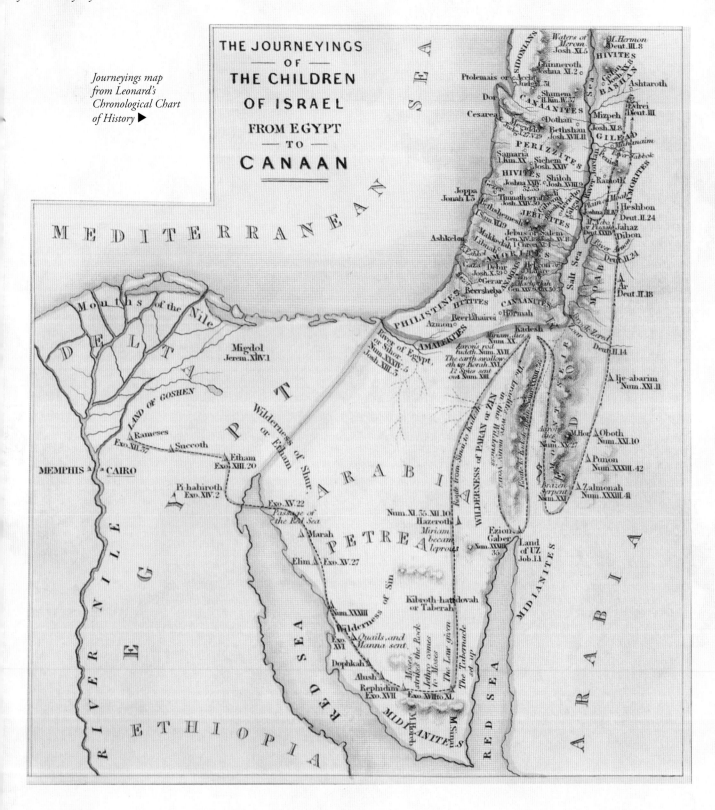

THE JOURNEYINGS
— OF —
THE CHILDREN
OF ISRAEL
FROM EGYPT
— TO —
CANAAN

THE KING'S HIGHWAY

Conquest of Canaan ▲   ▲ The Peak of Nebo

Chapter 8

INVASION

BEGINS

Because of their lack of faith God decreed that Israel would have to remain in the wilderness for 40 years and all except Caleb and Joshua would die. Archaeological evidence indicates that Israel spent this time in the Negev south of Beersheba. During this time Moses lost patience with the people and God decreed that he would not enter the Promised Land. The Israelites then resumed their journey passing Petra en route. Here Aaron died and was buried on Mount Hor. They defeated some kings on the way north including Barak who asked Balaam to pronounce a curse on Israel. Moses died before they crossed the Jordan River but he was resurrected and talked with Christ on the Mount of Transfiguration.

NUMBERS

TWO OF THE SPIES WHO HAD INSPECTED THE LAND, Joshua and Caleb, tried to encourage the people to believe that God could give them the land, but the people responded by threatening to stone them to death. "If only we had died in this wilderness!" they complained (Num. 14:2). God took them at their word and said that it would be another 40 years before they entered the Promised Land. Everyone except Joshua and Caleb would die before then.

Of course none of them really did want to die in the wilderness, so they decided they would proceed with an invasion anyway. Moses warned them against it but they persisted and launched an attack, only to be repulsed with heavy losses. They were obliged to spend 40 years in the wilderness where all that generation died.

The Bible does not reveal just where they spent that 40 years. Cohen identified many MBI sites to the northeast of Kadesh, but these were probably occupied after the conquest of Jericho.

Dr. Nelson Glueck found many MBI sites in the Negev south of Beersheba. Glueck was a devout American Jewish rabbi but maintained a close rapport with Arab Muslims in both Jordan and Israel. He was a brilliant archaeologist and in 1959 he wrote *Rivers in the Desert*, recording his archaeological investigations in the Negev in southern Israel.

DESERT WILDERNESS

The Negev is a rather inhospitable area with low rainfall and desert wastes, but thousands have eked out a living from its reluctant soil. For six years, under the auspices of the Hebrew Union College in America, Glueck scoured every inch of its hostile territory. He investigated and identified "more than a thousand ancient sites belonging to a whole series of advanced, agricultural civilizations existing in widely separated periods."[1]

He had a phenomenal memory and drew on records from secular sources, and he had tremendous confidence in what he called "the amazing historical memory of the Bible."[2]

In the early days of Canaan's history wildlife was very different from what it is today. "Monstrous rhinoceroses, hippopotami, elephants and cave oxen were common in this age. Their bones have been dug up all over the country from the Mediterranean coast to the Jordan River valley and in the mountain ranges in between. In the ancient bed of the Jordan, which is considerably below the present one, there was found an elephant's tusk six feet long. Bones and teeth of these great beasts have been discovered on the hills of Bethlehem."[3]

Glueck points out that Kadesh was on the western fringe of the Negev. From Kadesh, Moses had told the spies, "Go up this way into the South [Hebrew Negev] and go up to the mountains" (Num. 13:17). For their infidelity God said, "Your carcasses shall fall in this wilderness. And your sons shall be shepherds in the wilderness forty years" (Num. 14:32–33).

▼ *Nubian ibexes on a Mount Hor peak.*

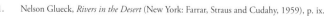

1. Nelson Glueck, *Rivers in the Desert* (New York: Farrar, Straus and Cudahy, 1959), p. ix.
2. Ibid., p. xi.
3. Ibid., p. 3.

▲ *Ancient Nabataean city in Israel's Negev Desert.*

▲ *Mount Hor, one of the traditional regions associated with the burial of Aaron.*

▲ *Moses Striking the Rock by Pieter de Grebber (1630).*

Most readers may assume that they turned back into the dreary wastes of the Sinai deserts, but is that assumption justified? Should all this MBI pottery in the Negev be interpreted to mean that the Israelites rather occupied the Negev? Of course, all this MBI ceramic evidence may have accrued after Israel conquered the Promised Land, but the possibility that this was where Israel spent those 40 years cannot be ruled out.

Glueck seemed to have been puzzled by "the fact that

plastered cisterns have not yet been found, for instance, in any site of the Middle Bronze Age."[4] If this was the time of the wilderness wandering in the Negev they would not need cisterns to collect the meager rainfall. The last recorded incident before they resumed their journey was at Kadesh where Moses became so exasperated with the complaining Israelites that he lost his temper and struck the rock instead of speaking to it as God had commanded. The water flowed, but for this lapse Moses was condemned to die before Israel entered the Land of Promise (Num. 20:1–13).

KING'S HIGHWAY

They journeyed eastward and Moses sent a message to the king of Edom, possibly in Petra, asking permission to proceed along the King's Highway. "We will not pass through fields or vineyards, nor will we drink water from wells; we will go along the King's Highway" (Num. 20:17). They even offered to pay for any water they used, but the request was met with a blunt refusal backed up by a show of military strength.

The road between Petra and Amman still goes by the name of King's Highway, and it follows the route used in antiquity. The Nabateans used it for trading, and later, when the province of Arabia was established in the second century A.D., the Roman Emperor Trajan remodeled the King's Highway and called it Via Nova Traiana. So the Israelites were obliged to take the dreary desert route to the east.

Before leaving the land of the Edomites, God told Moses to take Aaron and his son Eleazar to Mount Hor where Aaron was to hand over his priestly robes and then die. There is no certainty about the location of Mount Hor, but there is a mountaintop that can be seen from Petra that is claimed to be Mount Hor. A small Muslim monument

4. Ibid., p. 94.

The Prophet Balaam and the Ass, by Rembrandt van Rijn, 1626. ▶

crowns the summit and the belief is that here Aaron died and was buried.

To avoid confrontation with the Edomites, Israel "journeyed from Mount Hor by the way of the Red Sea" (Num. 21:4), but the desert route taxed the patience of many of the Israelites and again they complained to Moses. To divert their minds from such minor troubles God sent them a major problem — venomous snakes — and many of them died.

The remainder got the message and came to Moses confessing their sin and asking Moses to pray for them. In response to Moses' prayer, God told him to set up a pole with a bronze snake on it so that any who were bitten could look at the snake and be healed.

Jesus Christ referred to this incident when He was speaking with Nicodemus. He said, "As Moses lifted up the serpent in the wilderness, even so must the Son of Man be lifted up, that whoever believes in him should not perish but have eternal life" (John 3:14–15).

It may seem strange to some that a snake, the symbol of Satan, should be used to represent Christ, but Paul said in 2 Corinthians 5:21 that "He made Him who knew no sin to be sin for us, that we might become the righteousness of God in Him." He not only died for our sins, He became sin. The snake was a fitting symbol of sin.

As they continued their journey, the Israelites took the bronze serpent with them and it survived right down to the time of Hezekiah, 700 years later. By that time it had become an idolatrous symbol and people were burning incense to it, so Hezekiah had it broken in pieces (2 Kings 18:4).

THE BLESSING

The Israelites continued their journey north, defeating some local kings along the way, until they reached the hills opposite Jericho. King Barak had heard of their approach and their victories along the way. He concluded that he needed more than military might to resist these people who had a miracle-working God on their side, so he sent a message to a man by the name of Balaam to come and place a curse on the Israelites.

Balaam had been used by God as a prophet, but he had apostatized, though he still had a reputation, and Balak offered him rich rewards if he could bring about Israel's destruction. Balaam's

◀ *Moses was denied permission to travel this route. The road between Petra Amman still goes by the name of King's Highway.*

▲ *The Franciscan Church of the Transfiguration on Mount Tabor in Israel. Mount Tabor is traditionally identified as the Mount of Transfiguration. (Inset) Transfiguration by Lodovico Carracci, 1594, depicting Elijah, Jesus, and Moses with the three apostles.*

donkey was allowed to speak, and this eventually revealed the Lord's angel who instructed him to proceed to his destination. To Balak's disgust, when Balaam opened his mouth, God caused him to pronounce a blessing on Israel, not a curse.

It is an unusual story for the Bible, but it really happened and there is archaeological support for it. In 1967 a Dutch team was excavating a ruined building at Deir Alla in Jordan. They found some plaster fragments on the floor and noticed that there was some writing in red and black ink on them. They gathered 119 pieces, put them all together, and found the unusual name of Balaam and a prophecy he had made.

This inscription does not prove the Bible story of Balaam, but it does show that people still knew of Balaam 600 years after he lived. The inscription is now in the Amman Museum.

RESURRECTION

Israel was encamped on the plain on the east side of the River Jordan when Moses finished writing the Book of Deuteronomy. He then climbed to the top of Mount Nebo where, after viewing the Promised Land, he died a lonely death. But it was not for long. Paul wrote in Romans 5:14, that "death reigned from Adam to Moses."

Nobody had ever been raised from the dead since sin first entered the world, but "Michael the archangel, in contending with the devil, when he disputed about the body of Moses, dared not bring against him a reviling accusation, but said, 'The Lord rebuke you!' " (Jude 1:9). The devil protested at Moses being raised from the dead, but he was resurrected and, with Elijah, talked with Christ on the Mount of Transfiguration (Matt. 17:3).

DESTRUCTION OF JERICHO

Crossing the Jordan ▲   ▲ The Invasion

◀ *The Jordan River, the place Jesus was baptized, was 5 miles east of Jericho.*

CROSSING THE JORDAN

After Moses died Joshua led the people across the river Jordan, which was in flood at the time, but it was miraculously dammed up at Adam to allow the Israelites to cross. The first city that confronted them was Jericho where God made the walls to collapse and the Israelites destroyed the city by fire. Archaeologists have found plenty evidence of fallen walls and destruction by fire but as they date this to six hundred years before the Israelite invasion they claim there is no evidence to support the Bible record. The solution is to be found in the reduction of dates, which would place the invasion at the end of the Early Bronze Age.

JOSHUA

"AFTER THE DEATH OF MOSES THE SERVANT OF THE LORD, it came to pass that the LORD spoke to Joshua the son of Nun, Moses' assistant, saying: 'Moses my servant is dead. Now therefore, arise, go over this Jordan, you and all this people, to the land which I am giving to them'" (Josh. 1:1–2).

Under normal circumstances, that would not be a very hard assignment. The Jordan is only a narrow river and in places it was shallow enough to wade across, but it was the time of harvest (Josh. 3:15). This probably refers to the barley harvest that happens in April. This was the time of the latter rains and the river Jordan was in flood. There was no way two million people could get across this river while it was flooding the surrounding plains.

But God had the answer. The priests were to step right into the water with the ark of God on their shoulders. It was a step of faith but it worked. "The waters which came down from upstream stood still, and rose in a heap very far away at Adam. . . . And the people crossed over opposite Jericho" (Josh. 3:16).

Adam is the name of a small settlement 19 miles (30 km) north of Jericho. Here the River Jordan passes through a narrow ravine. Several times in the past one of the walls has collapsed and filled the valley, completely stopping the flow of water. The most recent incident happened in 1927, and another stoppage is recorded as happening in 1267.

THE DESTRUCTION OF JERICHO

Concerning Jericho, the Bible record is dramatic but clear. For six days the armies of Israel marched around the city solemnly blowing their trumpets, but on the seventh day they "marched around the city seven times. And the seventh time it happened, when the priests blew the trumpets, that Joshua said to the people, 'Shout, for the Lord has given you the city! . . .' So the people shouted when the priests blew the trumpets. And it happened when the people heard the sound of the trumpet, and the people shouted with a great shout, that the wall fell down flat. Then the people went up into the city, every man straight before him, and they took the city. And they utterly destroyed all that was in the city. . . . But they burned the city and all that was in it with fire" (Josh. 6:15–24).

Now if this happened it should be an archaeologist's paradise. Fallen walls, the city destroyed by fire, destruction of everything in the city, and the city subsequently uninhabited for centuries — the evidence should all be there, and it is, but at a different time than the dates allocated by archaeologists to the layers of occupation at Jericho.

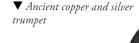

▼ *Ancient copper and silver trumpet*

The first major excavation at Jericho was by Professor John Garstang, who excavated from 1930 to 1936. He wrote:

The main defenses of Jericho in the Late Bronze Age followed the upper brink of the city mound, and comprised two parallel walls,

▲ *Remains of Jericho city walls, a city that many believe is the oldest continuously occupied town in the world.*

▲ *Burnt offerings uncovered at Jericho.*

▲ *Joshua and the Israelite people, Karolingischer Buchmaler, c.840.*

the outer six feet and the inner twelve feet thick. Investigations along the west side show continuous signs of destruction and conflagration. The outer wall suffered most, its remains falling down the slope. The inner wall is preserved only where it abuts the citadel, or tower, to a height of eighteen feet; elsewhere it is found largely to have fallen, together with the remains of buildings upon it, into the space between the walls which was filled with ruins and debris. Traces of intense fire are plain to see, including reddened masses of brick, cracked stones, charred timber and ashes. Houses alongside the wall were found burnt to the ground, their roofs fallen upon the domestic pottery within.[1]

In another room abutting the same western wall, but more to the south, the traces of fire upon its walls were as fresh as though it had occurred a month before; each scrape of the trowel exposed a black layer of charcoal, where the roof had burned, or caused the piled up ashes to run down in a stream. On a brick ledge in a corner of this room we found the family provision of dates, barley, oats, olives, an onion and peppercorns, all charred but unmistakable; while a little store of bread, together with a quantity of unbaked dough which had been laid aside to serve as leaven for the morrow's baking, told plainly the same tale of a people cut off in full activity.[2]

One gets used to burnt layers in excavations of this kind, for it was the usual fate of houses and cities to perish by fire; but this was no ordinary burning. The layer of ashes was so thick and the signs of intense heat so vivid, that it gave the

impression of having been contrived, that fuel had been added to the fire.[3]

Nothing could be more graphic or relevant to verify the Bible story, and Garstang attributed this destruction to the Late Bronze Period where archaeologists expected it to be, but then came Dr. Kathleen Kenyon. She excavated Jericho from 1952 to 1956 and felt obliged to write:

> We have nowhere been able to prove the survival of walls of the Late Bronze Age, that is to say of the period of Joshua. This is at variance with Professor Garstang's conclusions. He ascribed two of the lines of walls which encircle the summit to the Late Bronze Age. But everywhere that we examined them it was clear that they must belong to the Early Bronze Age, and have been buried beneath a massive scarp belonging to the Middle Bronze Age."[4]

ARCHAEOLOGICAL EVIDENCE

So Kenyon ascribed this evidence of destruction to the end of the Early Bronze Age, but according to Rudolph Cohen that's where it ought to be, and Kenyon's remarks about this period fit the biblical record exactly. This is what she wrote in her book *Archaeology in the Holy Land*:

> The final end of the early Bronze Age civilization came with catastrophic completeness. The last of the Early Bronze Age walls of Jericho was built in a great hurry, using old and broken bricks, and was probably not completed when it was destroyed by fire. Little or none of the town inside the walls has survived subsequent denudation, but it was probably completely destroyed, for all the finds

1. John Garstang and J.B.E. Garstang, *The Story of Jericho* (London: Marshall, Morgan & Scott, 1940), p. 136.
2. Ibid., p. 141.
3. Ibid., p. 142.
4. Kathleen Kenyon, *Digging Up Jericho* (New York: Praeger, 1957), p. 46.

▲ *Excavation of Jericho. (Inset) David Down points to the successive layers of occupation at Jericho.*

JOSHUA'S LEADERSHIP

Joshua had been one of the 12 spies Moses sent out from Kadesh Barnea. Joshua was 50 years old at the time. Joshua became Israel's leader at the age of 85 and led them for 25 years. He was dedicated to God and His Word, and he died at the age of 110 years.

show that there was an absolute break, and that a new people took the place of the earlier inhabitants. Every town in Palestine that has so far been investigated shows the same break. The newcomers were nomads, not interested in town life, and they so completely drove out or absorbed the old population, perhaps already weakened and decadent, that all traces of the Early Bronze Age civilization disappeared.[5]

"An absolute break . . . a new people . . . every town in Palestine . . . newcomers were nomads . . . completely drove out or absorbed the old population." Could we expect to find a more apt description of the Israelite invasion, nomads from the desert who initially were not interested in living in the cities?

The Israelites were a deeply religious people and consisted of 12 tribes. There is even evidence to confirm this. Kenyon wrote:

It can in any case be deduced that the newcomers were concerned with things spiritual from the care they took in the disposal of the dead. Probably long before they started to build houses they were excavating elaborate tombs in the rock of the surrounding hillsides. . . . The tombs fall into a number of sharply defined groups, which may be called the Dagger Tombs, the Pottery Tombs, the Square-shaft Tombs, an Outsize type which might be called the Bead type. . . . The newcomers had

5.   Kathleen Kenyon, *Archaeology in the Holy Land* (London: Ernest Benn Limited, 1965), p. 134.

a nomadic way of life when they arrived, and it seems to me that this differentiation can be explained as evidence of a number of tribal groups, each with its own burial custom, coming together as a loose tribal confederation, living side by side on the tell and the surrounding slopes, but each retaining its own burial customs.[6]

Other sites in Palestine have produced evidence that can also be interpreted as showing the presence of similar tribal groups.[7]

J.B. Pritchard, who excavated at Gibeon, came to the same conclusion. He stated:

These relics of the Middle Bronze l people seem to indicate a fresh migration into the town of a nomadic people who brought with them an entirely new tradition in pottery forms and new customs in burial practices. They may have come into Palestine from the desert at the crossing of the Jordan near Jericho and may then have pushed on to settle eventually at places such as Gibeon, Tell el-Ajjul and Lachish, where tombs of this distinctive type have been found.[8]

Nothing could more aptly fit the biblical record of the Israelites coming in from their desert wanderings, crossing the Jordan at Jericho, and occupying the Promised Land. Of particular interest is the evidence that these intruders were nomads. That aptly fits the Israelites, most of whom had been born in tents and lived in tents all their lives — and people who have always lived in tents do not want to live in cities.

For many centuries there were nomads in Jordan but there were two problems. First, it is almost impossible to tax people who are constantly on the move, and second, if any committed criminal offenses it was almost impossible to track them down. So King Hussein issued a law that all Bedouins had to move into houses, and as they pleaded that they could not afford to buy or build houses, the king provided houses for them. So they moved into the houses that had been provided for them, but guess what was in the back yard? Tents, of course. And what was in the houses? Their sheep and goats.

The migrating Israelites were nomads, and when they entered their Promised Land they had no disposition to occupy the houses of the cities they conquered. Of course, as time went by they were threatened by invaders and found it necessary to move into cities where they were protected by city walls, so in the MBII period we find evidence of city dwelling.

HOW ARCHAEOLOGY WORKS

To understand what this is all about, we need to know how

---

6.   Ibid., p. 194–195.
7.   Ibid., p. 207.
8.   J.B. Pritchard, *Where the Sun Stood Still* (Calabasas, CA: Toucan Pub., 1992), p. 153.

archaeology works and the basis for the traditional chronology.

In Israel, most of the cities in the pre-Christian era were built on low hills. Jesus referred to this practice when He said in the Sermon on the Mount, "A city that is set on a hill cannot be hidden" (Matt. 5:14).

There were three advantages in this custom. In the first place, it was better for defense. If an enemy had to scale a hill before attacking a city wall it made it more difficult for him. Then there were climatic reasons. In summertime they could catch the cool breezes, and in wintertime they would not be washed away by the heavy downpours of rain that often occur.

But in Israel we have the strange phenomenon of such cities rising in height. There were no garbage collectors, and debris was simply thrown out the front door, raising the height of the narrow street outside. In the course of time the house owner had to raise the height of his floor and the process started all over again.

Sometimes there was an earthquake that caused houses to collapse, or an enemy came and destroyed the houses. In each case, the residents would level off the debris and build on top. Over the centuries the top of such a hill might be 100 feet (30 m) or more above the original height of the hill. This gives archaeologists a golden opportunity to explore the past. By digging a shaft or a trench they can expose the ascending layers of occupation and reconstruct the history of the abandoned city.

Quite often the successive layers of occupation can be distinctly identified, and names have been attached to these strata. The lowest layer is called Early Bronze. The layer above that is Middle Bronze and above that is Late Bronze.

Finally there is the Iron Age. These layers in turn can be subdivided, so we have Early Bronze I, Early Bronze II, and Early Bronze III. No one will dispute the identification of these layers. The problem arises when dates are assigned to these periods.

The date often assigned to the beginning of the Early Bronze Age is 3100 B.C., but some scholars place it as early as 3400 B.C., while others choose a date as late as 2850 B.C. The Middle Bronze Age is dated about 2100 B.C., Late Bronze about 1550 B.C., and Iron Age about 1200 B.C., but herein is the problem with biblical history. As the Exodus and subsequent invasion of Canaan took place about 1405 B.C., we would expect to find evidence during the Late Bronze Period of the invading Israelites, but we don't.

A NEW PEOPLE

A new people coming into the country would inevitably bring with them a new style of pottery, new weapons, new tools, and different burial customs, but archaeologists digging down through the Late Bronze layers find no such evidence. The same type of people who occupied Canaan at the beginning of the Late Bronze Age seem to be the same type of people living there at the end of this period.

This problem led Dr. Israel Finkelstein, in his book *The Bible Unearthed*, to write, "It is now evident that the many events of biblical history did not take place in either the particular era or the manner described. Some of the most famous events in the Bible clearly never happened at all."[9]

However, the dates assigned to these archaeological

9.   Israel Finkelstein, *The Bible Unearthed* (New York: Free Press, 2001), p. 5.

▲ *The Church of the Beatitudes on the northern coast of the Sea of Galilee and is on a hill that rises near Capernaum, which is one of the possible locations for the Sermon on the Mount.*

strata are on the basis of synchronisms with Egyptian history, and some scholars are now of the opinion that these dates should be drastically reduced. This would result in a reduction of dates for the archaeological strata. The evidence for destruction at Jericho is correctly ascribed to the end of the Early Bronze Period, which should be redated to 1405 B.C., and that would be consistent with the Bible record. The Middle Bronze I people would be the Israelites who destroyed Jericho at the end of the Early Bronze Period and occupied the Promised Land.

▼ *Panaromic view of Jericho*

LAND BEYOND JERICHO

Attack on Ai ▲   ▲ Philistines in Gaza

Chapter 10

JOSHUA TO JUDGES

After destroying Jericho, Joshua attacked Ai. Following an initial defeat Ai was captured and remained unoccupied. By the traditional chronology archaeology contradicts this record but by a reduced chronology there is a prefect consistency. The Israelites then traveled to Shechem where they renewed their allegiance to God. Acoustic research has demonstrated that the priests could be heard by the huge assembly. Hazor was the next kingdom Israel conquered. The sanctuary was then set up at Shiloh. Today a platform cut out of the rocky hill can be seen. It exactly fits the dimensions of the ancient sanctuary compound. An army under Deborah and Barak defeated the Canaanites at Hazor and later Gideon with only 300 loyal soldiers routed the Midianites. Samson judged Israel for 40 years, but finally fell a victim to his weakness for women. He was betrayed by Delilah and ended his days turning a millstone.

JOSHUA

AFTER THE DRAMATIC CONQUEST OF JERICHO, THE less important city of Ai would seem to be a walkover. The spies Joshua sent out returned with the message, " 'Do not let all the people go up, but let about two or three thousand men go up and attack Ai' " (Josh. 7:3). It turned out to be bad advice. "The men of Ai struck down about thirty-six men" (Josh. 7:5), and the rest fled in disorder. The problem turned out to be the misconduct of Achan, so when this was attended to the Israelites made a successful attack on Ai, and "Joshua burned Ai and made it a heap [tell] forever, a desolation to this day" (Josh. 8:28).

Here, also, critical archaeologists seem to have a point. According to the Bible record, Ai was destroyed by fire and lay unoccupied for some time after. An abandoned city on a hill is called a "tell." By the chronology they cling to, most archaeologists would assign the biblical destruction of Ai to the Iron Age, but the archaeological evidence indicates that Ai was unoccupied at that time.

Dr. Amihai Mazar of the Hebrew University, in his book *Archaeology of the Land of the Bible*, wrote, "Between Beitin (Bethel) and the desert to the east, there is only one site which could have been referred to as 'Ai.' . . . A long gap in occupation followed the large Early Bronze Age city at Ai. . . . This lack of any Late Bronze Canaanite city at the site or in the vicinity contradicts the narrative in Joshua 8 and shows that it was not based on historical reality."[1]

But if Joshua's conquest is placed at the end of the Early Bronze Age, the evidence is fully supportive of the Bible — destruction followed by a gap in occupation. As Mazar pointed out, "A long gap in occupation followed the large Early Bronze Age city at Ai."

ACOUSTICS AND ARCHAEOLOGY

Before Moses died he instructed Israel to gather in the valley between Mount Ebal and Mount Gerizim for a ceremony of dedication. Six tribes were to stand on Mount Ebal and six on Mount Gerizim, and the Levites were to pronounce a list of curses on those who disregarded the divine precepts, and blessings on those who heeded them. The people assembled on the two mountains were to respond with fervent amens (Deut. 27:15). To make it so everyone could hear, the Levites were told to "speak with a loud voice" (Deut. 27:14).

Under normal circumstances, it would seem to require more than a loud voice to enable two million people to hear what the priests were saying. Two thousand years ago and earlier there were no public address systems, yet historical records tell of speakers addressing huge gatherings that apparently could distinctly hear what was being said. This required speakers with strong, resonant voices, and sites with outstanding acoustics.

B. Cobbey Crisler decided to enlist the latest technology to put the acoustics of

---

1.   Amihai Mazar, *Archaeology of the Land of the Bible* (New York: Doubleday, 1990), p. 331.

▲ *Tel Hazor provides some of the richest archaeological finds in Israel.*

▲ *The remains of Hazor, the ancient city between Ramah and Kadesh.*

some sites to the test, and he came up with some interesting results, as reported in *Biblical Archaeologist*. He conveyed his thoughts to the acoustical firm of Bolt, Beranek, and Newman in America, and they were so intrigued that they assigned one of their experts, Mark Myles, to the job. Both Mark and the company donated their time to the project.

One of the places they experimented on was Shechem, which nestles between Mount Gerizim and Mount Ebal at the south end of the Arab city of Nablus. This is today a noisy bustling city that would seem to preclude any possibility of a sound test, but it so happened that right beside Tell Balatah, ancient Shechem, was a factory emitting rhythmic and incessant metallic pounding, the sound of which could be isolated from the confused noise of the city.

Cobbey says, "We took sound level measurements of this syncopated metallic pounding . . . and proceeded to the head of Mount Gerizim. . . . A simple calculation based on the loudness of the sound source and the distance the sound had to travel indicated how loud it should have been at the head of the mountain. Our measurements agreed very well with the theory and showed that a human voice could have been heard clearly at Tell er-ras" (the peak of Mount Gerizim that can be seen from Shechem).[2]

DESTROYED BY FIRE

Far to the north, the king of Hazor heard of Joshua's conquests and was alarmed at the threat to his kingdom, so he appealed to his allies to confront the Israelite army. Joshua's army was successful in the ensuing battle and Joshua "burned Hazor with fire" (Josh. 11:11). Confirmation of the status of Hazor has been found. Hazor was "formerly the head of all those kingdoms" (Josh. 11:10).

Excavations at Hazor have demonstrated the validity of this statement. Hazor is the largest tell in Israel. There is an acropolis extending over 15 acres and a vast lower city

2.   B. Cobbey Crisler, "The Acoustics and Crowd Capacity of Natural Theaters in Palestine," *Biblical Archaeologist* (December 1976): p. 139.

measuring 170 acres. The city is in a very strategic position in the Huleh Valley on the route to the north. Recent excavations have uncovered a large and impressive Late Bronze palace cum temple on the acropolis, indicating the importance of Hazor in that period.

BUILDING A TABERNACLE

When Israel came to Mount Sinai, Moses had been given detailed instruction about the building of a small portable sanctuary where priests were to perform sacrificial rituals. It consisted of boards plated with gold and a waterproof roof of badger skins (Exod. 26:14), which probably means seal skins. They would be fully waterproof.

It had two compartments, the inner compartment being approximately 16 feet by 16 feet (5 m by 5 m), and the outer compartment 33 feet by 16 feet (10 m by 5 m). This building was surrounded by a courtyard 164 feet by 82 feet (50 m by 25 m), flanked by linen cloths.

When the political situation settled down, Joshua called an assembly at Shiloh "and set up the tabernacle of meeting there" (Josh. 18:1). Shiloh is geographically situated in the heart of Israel and would have been accessible to residents all over the country. On the side of the hill on which the city of Shiloh was built is a platform that has been cut out of the rock. I took a tape measure and stretched it from side to side. It measured 85 feet (26 m), just wide enough to comfortably accommodate the sanctuary courtyard.

The instructions given for the building of the sanctuary indicated that it was to be orientated east to west (Exod. 26:18–22). I also took a compass with me, and it indicated that this platform ran from east to west, as the Bible says.

Israel Finkelstein excavated Shiloh from 1981 to 1984, but because he held to the traditional chronology, he had difficulty interpreting what he found. He wrote, "Perhaps the most intriguing aspect of the Middle Bronze Age finds

at Shiloh is that, already in this period, there appears to have been a shrine at this site."[3] This was obviously the sanctuary erected by Joshua, but in his thinking it was before Israel arrived there. (See Appendix 1.)

LACK OF HOUSES

Something else puzzled him — a massive wall around the city, yet no evidence of houses. He wrote:

> The total lack of houses in the Middle Bronze Age settlement is also surprising. . . . The massive fortifications, including the great stone wall and the glacis, raise another question. Even if we assume people lived at Shiloh at this time, as at a regular habitation site, we would have to wonder how such a small population managed to execute such an impressive building operation. Calculating population density in the manner generally accepted today, no more than 400 people would have lived at a site of slightly more than four acres. Among these 400 people would be fewer than 100 men. Thus, people from all over the region must have

participated in the building activities at Shiloh — a possibility that casts an interesting light on the city's importance, perhaps as a cult site already in the Middle Bronze Age.[4]

Within the framework of the revised chronology it is not hard to reconstruct the scenario. The sanctuary was a temporary structure more like a tent, and those living in the city would have been the priests and their families, also probably living in tents as they were accustomed to doing before entering Canaan. But believers from all over Israel would flock to the site for religious ceremonies, and apparently they contributed their labors to erecting the fortifications around the city.

So Finkelstein would have us believe that all this evidence of cult activity was before the Israelites arrived on the scene, but it is unthinkable that Joshua would have chosen a site that was a center of Canaanite worship to locate the sanctuary. Israel had enough trouble avoiding such influences without locating their place of worship on a Canaanite holy place. But if we recognize that the Middle Bronze Age was the time of Israelite occupation, the circumstances

---

3.   Israel Finkelstein, *Biblical Archaeology Review* (January 1981): p. 34.

4.   Ibid.

◀ *Large pillars that still stand in the remains at Hazor.*

Excavations at the ancient city of Tel Megiddo, which overlooks the Valley of Armageddon, Israel. ▶

The Megiddo tunnel that allowed people to access fresh water without leaving the protection of the city. ▼

match the Bible record exactly. Joshua chose a virgin site not associated with heathen worship.

INVASIONS AND REPENTANCE

"When all that generation had been gathered to their fathers, another generation arose after them who did not know the Lord" (Judg. 2:10). "The children of Israel did evil in the sight of the Lord. They forgot the Lord their God and served the Baals and Asherahs" (Judg. 3:7). It is incredible that a nation with Israel's heritage of divine guidance should resort to idols, but that is human nature. As a result, God allowed a succession of neighboring nations to invade the land. When the Israelites repented and asked for divine help, God raised up noble leaders called judges to lead them to victories over their enemies.

Joshua had destroyed Hazor with fire but it was soon rebuilt, and Jabin led the Canaanites to oppress Israel. "So the Lord sold them into the hand of Jabin king of Canaan, who reigned in Hazor. The commander of his army was Sisera" (Judg. 4:2).

"Now Deborah, a prophetess, the wife of Lapidoth, was judging Israel at that time" (Judg. 4:4). She sent a message to Barak instructing him to raise an army of ten thousand men and take them to Mount Tabor. It seemed an inadequate force to oppose the large Canaanite army with its 900 fearsome chariots, and Balak agreed only on the condition that Deborah go with him. The prophetess agreed but predicted that the credit for killing Sisera would go to a woman, not to Barak (Judg. 4:9).

A FATAL BLOW

The resulting conflict turned out to be one of the many "Battles of Armageddon" that have been fought in the Plain of Jezreel. At the western end of the plain was the powerful city of Megiddo. Armageddon means "Hill of Megiddo." Eric H. Cline wrote a book called *The Battles of Armageddon* in which he lists 35 decisive battles that have been fought there during the course of history.

"And the Lord routed Sisera and all his chariots and all his army with the edge of the sword before Barak; and Sisera alighted from his chariot and fled away on foot" (Judg. 4:15). He made his way to the tribe of Kenites with whom his city was on friendly terms, and came to the tent of Jael.

She welcomed him and invited him into her tent and covered him with a blanket. Before resorting to sleep, Sisera took the precaution of asking Jael for a drink of water. This was not just to slake his thirst. The offer of water was interpreted as a gesture of friendship.

The request was granted and Sisera fell into a sound sleep. "Then Jael, Heber's wife, took a tent peg and took a hammer in her hand, and went softly to him and drove the peg into his temple" (Judg. 4:21). Women were usually the ones who drove the tent pegs into the ground for a newly erected tent, so she was well qualified to strike this fatal blow.

GIDEON'S ARMY

Yet again, "The children of Israel did evil in the sight of the Lord. So the Lord delivered them into the hand of Midian for seven years" (Judg. 6:1). When they appealed to God for divine help, God commissioned Gideon to round up an army to fight against their foe. Gideon initially rounded up 32,000 men.

They were encamped by the spring of Harod that flows out of the base of the east end of the hills of Gilboa. The final test was for his remaining men to cross the Brook Harod. Those who leisurely knelt down and drank deeply were discarded. The men who hastily scooped up some water in their hands and eagerly pressed on were chosen. In this way, Gideon's army was whittled down to 300 men, but God gave him a great victory that could only be ascribed to the providence of God, not to a large army.

SAMSON AND STRAW MEN

The Bible devotes four chapters to the exploits of Samson, the strong man of Israel who lived during the period of Philistine supremacy. His family lived in Zorah, not far from Gath where Goliath came from. Many people in that area seemed to have been of abnormal height. Some of these big men had six fingers and six toes (2 Sam. 21:20).

In 1984 archaeologists working at Ain Ghazal in Jordan announced the discovery of some "straw men" they had unearthed. The 20-inch (half-meter) high statues had a core of straw that was covered with clay and shaped to human form. The intriguing aspect of these quaint little straw men is that some of them had six fingers and six toes. Apparently it was not uncommon for this to happen 3,000 years ago.

As a youth, Samson would not listen to reason. He saw a Philistine girl in Timna and asked his parents to arrange a marriage with her. They remonstrated with him, urging him to marry an Israelite girl, but his only response was, "Get her for me, for she pleases me well" (Judg. 14:3).

The marriage was arranged but at the marriage supper his wife-to-be betrayed his trust and Samson walked out on her. Later on he had second thoughts about the matter and went down to Timna to consummate the marriage, only to find her father had married her off to the best man at his marriage supper. Samson retaliated by burning the Philistine crops. This angered the people of Timna, who "burned her and her father with fire" (Judg. 15:6). There was no such thing as being burnt at the stake in those days. They would probably have shut them in their house and set it on fire.

INTERESTING FINDS

In 1985 I was involved in the excavations at Timna under the direction of Dr. Amihai Mazar, a brilliant Israeli archaeologist with whom I have very friendly relations. In 1995 he published his findings in a book entitled *Timna, a Biblical City in the Sorek Valley.* At the time I worked there most of the volunteers came from Texas and I enjoyed their broad Texan accent. There was much evidence of Middle Bronze occupation, which in my thinking represents the Israelite period.

One discovery particularly intrigued me. Dr. Mazar describes it in his book:

Two human skeletons found under the burnt debris of stratum VII provide evidence of the

▼ *David Down standing by Jezreel stones similar to stonehenge*

▲ *The fertile valley of Jezreel bordered by Mount Carmel, (inset) Jezreel pottery*

building's violent end. One lay on the floor in the center of the hall, and the other had fallen over the sill of the hall's entrance, among the fallen bricks from the second floor. These were the remains of two Timnahites who probably were trapped in the fiery collapse of the building.[5]

There was plenty evidence of the whole city being destroyed by fire on several occasions, but it was unusual for just one house to be so thoroughly burnt. I was tempted to wonder if this was the house in which Samson's wife and her father perished. The only catch is that this building was dated to the Late Bronze Age, which would not fit anyone's chronology as far as Samson is concerned.

UNUSUAL WEAPON

On a subsequent occasion Samson was confronted by a thousand Philistines, and the record says that "he found a fresh jawbone of a donkey, reached out his hand and took it, and killed a thousand men with it" (Judg. 15:15). That may seem to be an unlikely weapon with which to slay so many foes, but on the Philistine coast archaeologists found such a jawbone with some sharp flint stones embedded in the inside curve. The inner end of the jaw would make a suitable handle. This jawbone had been used as a sickle, but as I viewed it in the Tel Aviv Museum I could well imagine how deadly a weapon it would have been in the powerful hand of Samson.

But a woman caused Samson's downfall. He fell in love with Delilah, but she betrayed him to the Philistines, who put out his eyes and took him down to Gaza where they put him to work grinding wheat into flour. Such a millstone is usually pulled around by an animal, blindfolded to prevent dizziness as it went round and round. This would have been the reason they put Samson's eyes out.

5.   George L. Kelm and Amihai Mazar, *Timna: a Biblical City in the Sorek Valley* (Winona Lake, IN: Eisenbrauns, 1995), p. 61.

Rembrandt's painting of Samson and Delilah (1628). ▶

BEIT SHE'AN

The Ark Captured ▲   ▲ Battle on Mount Gilboa

Roman ruins at Beit She'an, a city once ruled by Egypt, the Canaanites, Philistines, and eventually the Roman Empire.

SAMUEL AND SAUL

Hannah was a godly woman who dedicated her boy Samuel to the service of the sanctuary. Eli was the high priest at the time. War with the Philistines broke out and they captured the Ark of the Covenant and took it to their cities. A plague broke out and they sent the sacred ark back to Israel. Samuel became the judge of Israel but the people clamored for a king. A tall man named Saul was chosen but he presumed to offer a sacrifice which only the priests were authorized to offer, and Saul was rejected. The young shepherd boy David was chosen in his place. Subsequently David was appointed to play sweet music to soothe Saul's troubled nerves. David showed his worth by killing Goliath in the Valley of Elah. Saul became jealous of David who had to escape to the hills. Finally Saul and his sons were killed in the battle with the Philistines on the Hills of Gilboa.

HANNAH WAS A GODLY WOMAN WHO WAS BARREN, but she promised God that if a child was born to her she would dedicate him to the service of the sanctuary. Her prayer was answered and when Samuel was weaned, which was probably when he was about two or three years of age, Hannah took him to Eli the high priest at Shiloh.

Eli was a fat old man, partially blind, and 98 years of age when Israel made war with the Philistines and lost. Thinking that the presence of the ark containing the two tablets of stone on which were written the Ten Commandments might have some magical qualities, the army sent for the ark to be brought to the battlefield. The result was disastrous. The Israelite army suffered another defeat, Eli's two sons were killed, and the Philistines took possession of the ark.

ELI'S DEATH

A messenger brought the news to Shiloh. "There was Eli, sitting on a seat by the wayside" (1 Sam. 4:13). This expression is significant. The road into Shiloh winds around the side of the hill and past the site of the sanctuary before entering the city. Eli would have been sitting beside the sanctuary when the messenger arrived. When Eli heard that the sacred ark had been captured he was so shocked he fell off his stool and broke his neck.

The triumphant Philistines took the ark to Ashdod, a city near the Mediterranean coast, and installed it in the temple of Dagon, a known pagan deity with human head and a fish body. When the image of Dagon repeatedly fell, the Philistines sent it to Gath where an epidemic broke out, so they sent it to Ekron, which was similarly infected by an epidemic.

The nature of this affliction has been much debated. The Bible says, "He struck the men of the city, both small and great, and tumors broke out on them" (1 Sam. 5:9).

AFFLICTED CITIES

Aren M. Maeir recently excavated at Tell es Safi, now identified as Gath, and he wrote an article that was published in the May 2008 edition of *Biblical Archaeology Review*. He points out that the Hebrew word translated tumors is *opalim,* related to Ophel the upper city of Jerusalem, and means high or rise. He suggests that as this was something that afflicted the men of the city, it affected their ability to gain an erection.

In some areas it was common practice to make a model of the infected part of the anatomy — legs, arms, ears, etc. — that might be infected and bring them to the temple asking for a cure. In Gath, Maeir found two clay objects that undoubtedly represented the male organ in erection. As a trespass offering, the Philistine lords sent "five golden tumors [opalim] and five golden rats" with the ark (1 Sam. 6:4). That does not explain why models of the rats were sent unless they suspected them of being carriers of the disease.

▼ *David Down standing near the Bethshan gate.*

▲ *Gate system at Tel Beth-Shemesh, Dustinroyer (CC-BY-3.0).*

▲ *The gate of Beth Shan, the city where the Philistines displayed King Saul's body from the walls.*

The site of Ekron was not positively identified until 1957 when Joseph Naveh proposed that Tel Miqne should be identified as Ekron. Seymour Gitin and Trude Dothan conducted excavations there from 1981 to 1986. As it was only a low hill, it had not even been identified as an abandoned city. The excavations revealed no less than 102 olive oil presses capable of producing a thousand tons of oil every year, indicating that this must have been a lucrative export industry.

PHILISTINE HISTORY

The origin of the Philistines has been grossly misunderstood. Conclusions have been drawn from the reliefs on the walls of the temple of Rameses III at Medinet Habu in Egypt. Rameses III was supposed to have ruled in the 12th century B.C., but the enemy warriors depicted have what seem like feathered helmets and are called "Pereset," which archaeologists have interpreted to mean "Philistines." They say they were part of the coalition army that invaded Egypt at this time, and that this was when the Philistines first became established along the Mediterranean coast.

However, Abraham had dealings with the Philistines hundreds of years earlier (Gen. 21:34), as did his son (Isa. 26:1), and when the exodus occurred in 1445 B.C., God told the Israelites that He would not lead them by way of the Philistines (Exod. 13:17). All of this clearly demonstrates that the Philistines were there long before the time of Rameses III.

Actually, the feathered helmets are typical of Persian soldiers, and Rameses III should be dated to the Persian period. So all the so-called knowledge we have of the Philistines, their origins, and their peculiar helmets has been totally misrepresented. We really know very little about the Philistines of biblical times. They left no inscriptions and all we really know of them has to be derived from the Bible, Assyrian inscriptions, and archaeology.

ARK AND ABU GHOSH

The Philistines decided that the ark of God was too dangerous to keep and sent it on an ox cart to Beth Shemesh. When the residents of this city impiously looked inside the ark they were smitten by a plague, and they sent the ark to Kirjath Jearim where it remained for 20 years. This location is now known as Abu Ghosh and a Roman Catholic church stands on the site. On the roof of the church is a replica of the ark with a statue of the virgin Mary standing on the ark.

In the meantime, Shiloh had been conquered and destroyed, and we find Samuel residing at Ramah only nine miles (15 km) north of Jerusalem. Up until this time Israel had preserved its identity as a theocracy ruled by judges and prophets, but the people began to clamor for a king to be like the nations around them. God told Samuel to accede to their demands and anoint Saul, a noble man of imposing height. It seemed a good choice, but time was to reveal defects in his character.

At this time the Philistines were a major force in the region and mustered a huge army to attack Israel. "Then the Philistines gathered together to fight with Israel, thirty thousand chariots and six thousand horsemen, and people as the sand which is on the seashore in multitude. And they came up and encamped at Michmash" (1 Sam. 13:5).

Apparently Samuel had promised to come to bless the army of Israel and had told Saul to wait for his arrival. Saul waited seven days, but as Samuel had not shown up, Saul took it on himself to offer a burnt offering. This he was not authorized to do, and when Samuel arrived he took a serious view of Saul's deviation from divine instructions.

And Samuel said to Saul, "You have done foolishly. You have not kept the commandment of the Lord your God. . . . Now your kingdom shall not continue. The Lord has sought for Himself a man after His own heart" (1 Sam. 13:13–14).

Subsequently, Samuel commissioned Saul to destroy the Amalekites, who had so basely attacked the Israelites as they left Egypt. At that time God had said, "'Write this for a memorial in the book and recount it in the hearing of Joshua, that I will utterly blot out the remembrance of Amalek from under heaven'" (Exod. 17:14).

By a reduced chronology, the Amalekites should be identified as the Hyksos who invaded Egypt and, according to the Egyptian priest Manetho, "occupied it without a battle." They could only achieve this because the Egyptian army was at the bottom of the Red Sea. They would have heard from the Israelites they had captured in battle how Pharaoh and all his army had perished in the Red Sea and could have seized the opportunity to invade the country.

Now the time for retribution had come. Samuel had instructed Saul to "kill both man and woman, infant and nursing child, ox and sheep, camel and donkey" (1 Sam. 15:3). Saul was highly successful and "utterly destroyed all the people with the edge of the sword" (1 Sam. 15:8).

When the Egyptians revolted against the Hyksos they drove them out of Egypt, and they migrated to Sharuhen in southern Canaan. Archaeologists are puzzled over what happened to them then. There is no further record of them.

The answer could lie in the biblical records. If the Hyksos were the Amalekites destroyed by Saul, it is not surprising that they seem to disappear from history.

But the Israelites could not resist the temptation to spare the best of the flocks and herds on the pretext that they were going to offer them as sacrifices to the Lord. This no doubt saved them from having to offer their own flocks in sacrifices.

For this dereliction of duty Saul was rejected as king of Israel. Samuel sternly told Saul, "'To obey is better than sacrifice. . . . The Lord has rejected you from being king over Israel'" (1 Sam. 15:22–26).

SHEPHERD BOY TO KING

Samuel was then sent to Bethlehem to anoint the young shepherd boy David in his stead. Saul was unaware of David's selection but became quite morose at the realization that God had rejected him. He became so despondent that his servants recommended that a musician be found to play sweet music to soothe his troubled mind. They recommended young David, who was skillful on the lyre.

David had probably already composed some psalms such as Psalm 23, "The Lord is my shepherd, I shall not want," and he now played soothing music to calm Saul's troubled nerves. Saul was pleased with David and made him his armorbearer (1 Sam. 16:21).

But the Philistines still posed a threat to Israel and once more challenged the armies of Israel. Both sides were drawn up on hills on opposite sides of the Valley of Elah, and for 40 days there was a standoff. Neither side was eager to make the first move, which would place them at a disadvantage. The army initiating an offensive would have to descend to the plain and expose themselves to the other army, which would be able to swarm down their hill onto the enemy below them.

While this stalemate continued, a champion of the Philistine host hurled a daily challenge at the Israelites. His name was Goliath and he was about ten feet (three m) in height.

Goliath came from the Philistine city of Gath (1 Sam.

◀ *David and Goliath, a color lithograph by Osmar Schindler (c. 1888)*

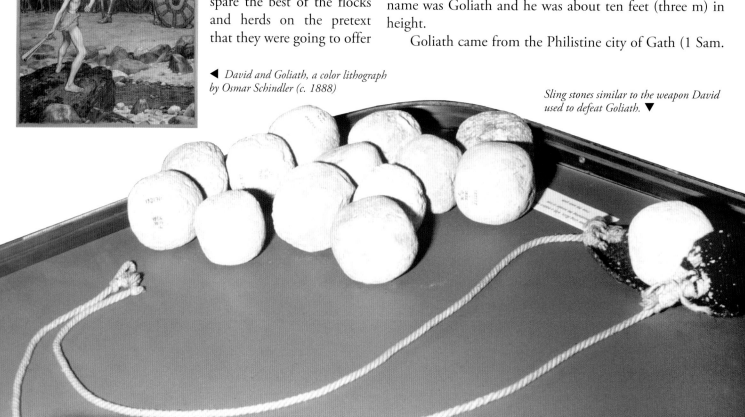

Sling stones similar to the weapon David used to defeat Goliath. ▼

▲ *The Gilboa hills above the Jezreel Valley.*

17:4), but until 2004 Gath had not been positively identified. In that year a team from the Bar Ilan University in Tel Aviv commenced excavations on a tell called Tel es Safar and found evidence that this was indeed the ancient city of Gath. More than that, they even unearthed an ostracon on which the name "Goliath" was scratched.

An ostracon is a piece of pottery used for writing. Common writing materials were papyrus and vellum (animal skins), but these cost money, so for writing receipts, keeping notes, or scribbling a love letter, broken pottery was readily available and proved to be suitable for writing on. No one is suggesting that this ostracon referred to the biblical Goliath, but it did show that Goliath was a known name in Gath.

Each morning Goliath stood in the plain and shouted to the Israelites, "I defy the armies of Israel this day; give me a man, that we may fight together" (1 Sam. 17:10). Saul was head and shoulders above his compatriots, but he was not about to take up the challenge against this formidable giant.

It was the responsibility of the soldiers to provide for their own necessities, and as David had three brothers in the army their father sent young David with food supplies for them. On reaching the battle scene David heard Goliath's defiant challenge and expressed his indignation. His words were reported to Saul, who offered David his own personal armor to go and fight Goliath, but David preferred his trusty sling.

Winding its way through the valley was a wadi, a small riverbed that flowed with water when it rained but was dry in summertime. In the bed of this wadi were innumerable stones rounded by being washed down the wadi bed. David selected "five round stones" and put them in his shepherd's bag.

Then he made a very strategic move. "David hurried and ran toward the army to meet the Philistine" (1 Sam. 17:48). David's stone sped straight at the giant's head, struck him in the forehead, and brought him to the ground. David seized Goliath's sword and severed his head.

Rechavam Ze'evy, a retired general of the Israeli army, believes it all actually happened. As an experienced officer he has closely analyzed every aspect of the confrontation and concludes that it is all very plausible.

Rechavam was interviewed by journalist Yadin Roman, who wrote it up in *Eretz,* the Israeli equivalent of America's *National Geographic* magazine. They stood on the side of the Valley of Elah as they discussed the logistics of the battle. "He has no doubts about the historicity of the battle," Yadin Roman wrote. "It happened, and a military man can evaluate its purpose, course, and outcome."

For Rechavam, "The Philistine's ancient strategy is textbook material. He who holds the highlands and

Israelite was running to meet him and he awaited the next move. That was David's chance — a stationary target — and he flung his stone, which became embedded in his opponent's forehead. The biblical account seems to record an inconsequential detail, but to the military man it is full of significance.

Rechavam then asks, "The battle's over. So what? What do you do, get your picture into the media, give an interview, and that's it? That's a mistake. You take advantage of victory by attacking the disarrayed forces of the enemy." The Bible says, "Now the men of Israel and Judah arose and shouted, and pursued the Philistines as far as the entrance of the valley and to the gates of Ekron" (1 Sam. 17:52).

Rechavam became a respected member of the Knesset, Israel's parliament. He is not an unquestioning Orthodox believer in the Bible, but to him the story of the famous battle makes military sense.

A KING'S ANGER

As Saul watched this drama unfold he inquired of Abner his army commander, "Whose son is this youth?" (1 Sam. 17:55). This question did not imply that Saul did not know David, for David had been playing sweet music to the king for some time, but lineage was very important in Bible times, and either Saul did not know who David's father was or he had forgotten, so he asked, "Whose son is this youth?"

David's victory did not bring the expected approbation from Saul. David led his group of soldiers in successful raids on Philistine garrisons and became popular with the people of Israel. So much so that the maidens sang, "Saul has slain his thousands, and David his ten thousands" (1 Sam. 18:7). When this came to Saul's ears it did not go down well with him, and he wanted to kill David.

This would not have been acceptable to the Israelites, so Saul hit on a subtle plan. He offered his daughter in marriage to David but required as a dowry 100 Philistine foreskins (1 Sam. 18:25). Saul secretly hoped that in the process David would lose his life, but the plan did not work. David was highly successful and killed 200 Philistines and "brought their foreskins, and they gave them in full count to the king" (1 Sam. 18:27).

This may seem rather crude to Western readers, but it was common practice in those days. No male would part with that part of his anatomy so long as he lived, so the presentation of these emblems guaranteed that the men

mountains controls the lowlands and the coast. It's a lesson we teach in every military command course."

Rechavam makes an interesting observation about the duel. He points out that Goliath was lacking one major weapon of the times. "He doesn't have a bow. His fighting ability has no range." On the other hand, David does. He has his sling, and as Rechavam points out, "I know Bedouin shepherds who can hit a tin can with a stone flung from a sling from a distance of seventy-five metres."[1]

But there is a difference between a tin can and a Philistine giant — one is stationary and the other mobile. So David has to immobilize his target, and this is where Rechavam brings out another fine point that a civilian would miss. The record says that "David hastened and ran toward the army to meet the Philistine" (1 Sam. 17:48).

That stopped the Philistine in his tracks. The young

---

1.   Yadin Roman, *Eretz* (July 1998).

▲ *Stone steps leading to the city of Beth Shemesh.*

▲ *The coastline of the Mediterranean Sea from Ashkelon.*

had been killed. On the walls of Medinet Habu in Egypt scribes can be seen counting out these objects and placing them in a pile.

Saul became so hostile to David that the latter was obliged to flee. He even took refuge in Gath, a Philistine city, but later fled to Engedi by the Dead Sea. Here is a copious spring that could have provided enough water for David and his followers. Also, "David and his men went up to the stronghold" (1 Sam. 24:22). The Hebrew word used here for stronghold is *Metsodah*, which probably refers to Masada. So David would have been the first one to occupy this strategic fortress.

A final showdown between Saul and the Philistines came on the hills of Gilboa at the east end of the Valley of Jezreel. Saul was filled with trepidation at the prospect, and as God would not answer his prayers because of his evil life, "Saul said to his servants, 'Find me a woman who is a medium, that I may go to her and inquire of her' " (1 Sam. 28:7). This is the first recorded spiritualist séance in history.

In the Mosaic Law, mediums had been banned. "There shall not be found among you . . . one who conjures spells, or a medium, or a spiritist, or one who calls up the dead" (Deut. 18:10–11). The witch of Endor was rather wary, but when Saul assured her of judicial immunity she asked him, "Whom shall I bring up for you?" (1 Sam. 28:11).

Saul asked for Samuel and a form appeared that Saul took to be Samuel, but it was certainly not the dead prophet. God would not have sent his prophet to Saul when "the Lord did not answer him,

either by dreams or by Urim or by the prophets" (1 Sam. 28:6). It was more likely an evil spirit impersonating Samuel.

In the battle on Mount Gilboa, Saul and his sons were killed. The Philistines fastened Saul's body to the wall of the nearby city of Beth Shan. In the Middle Bronze Age, Beth Shan was a major city in Israel and sat astride a very prominent hill in the Jordan Valley. Excavations there by Dr. Amihai Mazar have uncovered much archaeological evidence of the period in which this all happened.

▼ *Map of Canaan from Leonard's Chronological Chart of History.*

LEGACY OF DAVID

Ruling from Hebron ▲

▲ Solomon Becomes Co-regent

Chapter 12

DAVID AS KING

After Saul died David became king in Hebron for seven years. He then captured Jerusalem and reigned there for 33 years. The Philistines were alarmed at this move and marched toward Jerusalem.

David defeated them in the Valley of Rephaim. He then brought the ark of the Covenant to Jerusalem. He later conquered the Ammonites, Edomites, and Syrians, extending his empire to the Euphrates River. Archaeologists who cling to the traditional chronology place this period in the Iron Age and point out that this was a period of comparative poverty. True, but by the revised chronology this would have been during the Middle Bronze Period which all archaeologists recognize as the most powerful and affluent period ever known in the Levant. King David has left us a priceless legacy in the psalms he wrote.

ON THE DEATH OF SAUL, THE KINGDOM OF ISRAEL passed into the hands of David, who ruled for seven years in Hebron. Then David decided to make Jerusalem his capital city. At this time Jerusalem was strategically located on a spur of land to the south of the present Old City of Jerusalem, then known as Jebus. It would have been well defended by a strong wall around the top of the spur that David surmised would be unconquerable, but Jerusalem's water supply has always come from the Gihon Spring, which flowed out from beneath the city.

A shaft would have provided the women access to this water supply. David surmised that this would be the surest way into the city and promised that anyone of his army who climbed up this shaft and gained access to the city would be made commander-in-chief of the army. Joab accepted the challenge and succeeded in capturing the city.

In 1867 Charles Warren went to Palestine and found a shaft located above the spring and concluded it was the shaft that Joab had climbed, but this would have been almost impossible to scale and there were no rope marks in the sides of the shaft, implying that the women had not let down their water vessels here. However, in 1998 Ronny Reich found a stone tower-like structure that he concluded was the well-fortified shaft referred to in the Bible record.

OLD ENEMIES THREATEN

The Philistines had become alarmed at David's adoption of Jerusalem as his capital city "and deployed themselves in the Valley of Rephaim" (2 Sam. 5:18). This valley extends from the west of Jerusalem right down to the Philistine plains. *Rephaim* in Hebrew means "giants," and there were giants in the Philistine army.

David repulsed them but they returned to threaten Israel again. David was apprehensive about facing this powerful army and inquired of the Lord, who advised him, "When you hear the sound of marching in the tops of the mulberry trees, then you shall advance quickly" (2 Sam. 5:24). A better translation would be "balsam trees" as given in the RSV version. David followed the directions given and repulsed the Philistines as far as Gezer in the plains. He was never again troubled by the Philistine armies.

David's next move was to bring the ark from the home of Abinadab in Kirjath Jearim to Jerusalem. It was a commendable project but it ended in disaster. The ark was set on a new cart, but the road was rough and the ark was in danger of falling off. Uzzah put out his hand to steady the ark but was immediately struck dead for his impiety.

This judgment on Uzzah seems rather harsh, but the problem was that neither David nor Uzzah had done his homework. They had failed to study the Scriptures to find out how it should have been done. The ark had poles through rings in the sides of the ark and should have been carried on the shoulders of the Levites. Israel had been warned against touching the ark with their hands (Num. 4:15), and although Uzzah's motives were commendable, he paid the price for his disregard of the divine command.

◄ *Statue that towers over Kirjath Jearim.*

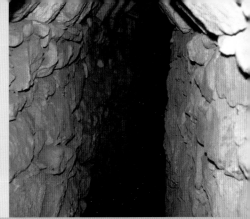

▲ Digs in the valley of Rephaim.　　▲ Entryway to Warren's Shaft in Jerusalem.　　▲ In Warren's Shaft, which led near the Gihon Spring.

FOLLOWING INSTRUCTIONS

At first David was displeased with the aborted attempt to bring the ark to Jerusalem, but as the result of some Bible study, he realized his mistake and subsequently had the ark brought safely to Jerusalem. "Then David said, 'No one may carry the ark of God but the Levites, for the Lord has chosen them to carry the ark of God" (1 Chron. 15:2).

Then David turned his attention to foreign policy. He launched successful wars against the Ammonites in the east, the Edomites in the south, and Syria in the north until his empire extended as far as the Euphrates River.

Most archaeologists in Israel dispute the accuracy of this record. By the traditional chronology David would have ruled in the Iron II period, and admittedly there is scant proof there for a powerful and affluent empire in Israel at that time.

Prominent Israeli archaeologists Israel Finkelstein and Neil Silberman wrote a book entitled *David and Solomon* in which they scoff at the biblical record. They wrote, "Many of the famous episodes in the biblical story of David and Solomon are fictions, historically questionable, or highly exaggerated."[1] They describe David's era as "a local dynasty of rustic tribal chiefs."[2]

As for Jerusalem, "The archaeological data from Jerusalem have shown that the settlement of the tenth century B.C.E. was no more than a small, poor highland village."[3]

They are obliged to admit, "The text seems to preserve some uncannily accurate memories of tenth century B.C.E. conditions. . . . The sheer weight of geographical information and long lists of place-names interwoven in its stories testify to a familiarity with the ancient landscape of Judah and Israel."[4]

So get it straight. Cling to the traditional chronology and you can scrap the Bible record, but if we recognize that the Middle Bronze II period was the time of David and Solomon, the evidence is compelling. Finkelstein and Silberman will tell you that.

In the Middle Bronze Age six or seven centuries before the estimated time of David, massive walls and towers of an impressive city. Fortification were built on the eastern slope of the city of David.[5]

FURTHER EVIDENCE

Of course there were the minimalists who went even further and denied that David ever really existed, but then came the Dan inscription. Avraham Biran started excavations in Dan in 1966 and spent just about the rest of his life there. In 1994 he published his book *Biblical Dan* in which he described this exciting discovery. It was a fragment of a slab of stone that he says could not be later than "the third quarter of the 8th century B.C.E."[6]

The minimalists were infuriated and some went so low as to accuse Biran of forging the inscription, but rational archaeologists admit that David must have been known at least that early in history.

Adherence to the traditional chronology has led some Israeli archaeologists to a rather curious conclusion. They place the beginning of the Jewish nation at the beginning of the Iron Age I period, 1200 B.C., but at that time there is no evidence for a new people coming into the country, so they are forced to the conclusion that the Israelites were just a breakaway group of Canaanites who developed into the Jewish nation.

In his book *The Archaeology of the Israelite Settlement*, Finkelstein says:

We accept that there must be a kernel of historical

1.　Israel Finkelstein and Neil Asher Silberman, *David and Solomon* (New York: Free Press, 2006), p. 21.
2.　Ibid., p. 22.
3.　Ibid., p. 80.
4.　Ibid., p. 33.

5.　Ibid., p. 274.
6.　Avraham Biran, *Biblical Dan* (Jerusalem: Israel Exploration Society; Hebrew Union College-Jewish Institute of Religion, 1994), p. 277.

◀ *A Stele (inscribed stone) found in Dan with inscription referring to the House of David.*

that he would eventually pay the penalty for his sins.

David was sincerely repentant and wrote two penitential psalms in which he acknowledged his guilt in the sight of God and his whole nation. He wrote, "I acknowledged my sin to You, and my iniquity I have not hidden" (Ps. 32:5). In perpetual remorse he wrote, "I acknowledge my transgressions, and my sin is always before me" (Ps. 51:3). He pleaded, "Have mercy upon me, O God, according to Your loving kindness; according to the multitude of Your tender mercies, blot out my transgressions" (Ps. 51:1). This was the attitude that made him a man after God's own heart.

His repentance was accepted by God. When the prophet Nathan boldly accused him of his shameful deeds, David immediately admitted, "I have sinned against the Lord" (2 Sam. 12:13). There was no waiting, no period of probation. Nathan promptly said, "The Lord also has put away your sin." That is the way the plan of salvation works. Instant forgiveness for the repentant sinner.

But retribution came all too soon. His own son Absalom, supported by David's former trusted counselor Ahithophel, revolted against him. Actually, Ahithophel had an axe to grind. He was the grandfather of Bathsheba and naturally resented David killing her husband, who was a loyal soldier of Hittite origin (2 Sam. 11:3, 23:34).

It was David's ambition to build a temple for God, but this privilege was denied him. Instead the prophet Nathan told him that his son would build the temple (2 Sam. 7:13). David had to be content with gathering the materials for

veracity in the deeply rooted tradition concerning the origin of Israel in Egypt. . . . At the same time, we cannot brush aside the possibility that certain groups who settled in the hill country in Iron I originated directly from the Canaanite society of the lowlands. . . . But the vast majority of the people who settled in the hill country and in Transjordan during the Iron I period must have been indigenous. . . . The process lasted about two centuries and culminated in the political consolidation and the national identity of Israel.[7]

So much for Abraham, Isaac, and Jacob, and the Exodus!

BEGGING MERCY

Unfortunately, David spoiled his copybook by committing adultery with Bathsheba and having her noble husband killed so he could marry her. The prophet Nathan let him know what God thought about the matter and predicted

---

7. Israel Finkelstein, *The Archaeology of the Israelite Settlement* (Jerusalem: Israel Exploration Society, 1988), p. 348.

DAVID'S RULE

David enlarged his kingdom and brought it to the peak of political and military power. He was king of Israel for 40 years. God promised that David's house and David's kingdom would remain before him forever (2 Samuel 7:8–16).

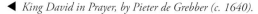
King David in Prayer, by Pieter de Grebber (c. 1640).

written in acrostic form. Four chapters have 22 verses and one has 66, a multiple of 22. Each verse commences with a consecutive letter of the alphabet.

David wrote nine acrostic psalms, though not all contained all 22 letters. The longest was Psalm 119, which has 176 verses, eight for each letter of the alphabet. Until recently it was thought that Psalm 145 was imperfect, as there were only 21 verses. The letter N was missing between verses 13 and 14, but recently a Dead Sea Scroll scholar noticed that one of the scrolls contained the missing verse. It should read, "God is faithful and glorious in all his deeds." Future printings of the Bible will include this verse.

the project.

Toward the end of his reign, David's son Adonijah attempted a coup to snatch the throne ahead of Solomon. David pre-empted this by crowning Solomon as his co-regent (1 Sam. 1:39).

DAVID'S LEGACY

Perhaps David's greatest legacy to us is the psalms he wrote. Psalms are songs accompanied by musical instruments. With David it was his beloved harp, which should be understood to be a lyre. Full-size harps were used in Egypt but obviously David could not have taken such an instrument with him while he tended his sheep.

Nearly half the 150 psalms in the Book of Psalms were written by David. The others were written by Moses, Solomon, and other authors. The Hebrew people were fond of poetry that was of a different nature than Western poetry, which has rhyme and rhythm. Hebrew poetry had repetition and contrast and other poetic forms. Actually, about one-third of the entire Old Testament is poetic.

A common form was the acrostic, of which David wrote nine. Many Western children were taught A is for apple, B is for ball, C is for cat, and D is for dog. A Hebrew acrostic follows the same pattern. There were 22 letters in the Hebrew alphabet. The whole Book of Lamentations is

Part of the large stone structure thought by some archaeologists to be the remains of King David's palace. ▶

REIGN IN JERUSALEM

The Royal Wedding ▲   A Fleet at Ezion Geber ▲

Chapter 13

GLORIES OF SOLOMON

Before his death King David crowned Solomon as the next king of Israel and Solomon married Pharaoh's daughter. This bride was probably Neferbiti, the daughter of Pharaoh Thutmosis I and sister of Queen Hatshepsut. David wrote a wedding song for the occasion, and Solomon wrote the Song of Songs to be sung at the wedding. Solomon went on to marry seven hundred wives and three hundred concubines. Many of these wives worshiped pagan gods and led Solomon to also worship false gods. Solomon's kingdom became fabulously wealthy and it extended from Egypt in the south to Palmyra on the north. Traditionally archaeologists place Solomon's reign in the Iron Age II Period and as this was a period of poverty they discredit the Bible record. The revised chronology would place Solomon in the Middle Bronze II Period which was an era of great affluence. God gave Solomon great wisdom and he built the magnificent temple in Jerusalem. Solomon was visited by the Queen of Sheba who should probably be identified with Queen Hatshepsut of Egypt.

AS DAVID'S END DREW NEAR, A MARRIAGE WAS arranged for Solomon, his son and heir. For this significant occasion David wrote a touching wedding song. "My heart is overflowing with a good theme," he wrote. To the bridegroom he said, "I recite my composition concerning the King. . . . In your majesty ride prosperously" (Ps. 45:1–4).

Solomon's bride was Pharaoh's daughter (1 Kings 3:1). By the revised chronology I advocate, this pharaoh would be Thutmosis I, and his daughter would be Neferbity, sister of Queen Hatshepsut. This daughter suddenly vanishes from Egyptian records and it is assumed that she died prematurely, but since there is no actual record of her death it is more likely that she married King Solomon.

Pharaoh gave a rather unusual marriage gift to Solomon on the occasion of his marriage to Pharaoh's daughter. "Pharaoh king of Egypt had gone up and taken Gezer and burned it with fire, had killed the Canaanites who dwelt in the city, and had given it as a dowry to his daughter, Solomon's wife" (1 Kings 9:16).

Israel had been told to completely occupy all the land of Canaan and to kill all its inhabitants, but they had failed to complete this task. The Canaanite occupants of Gezer had survived and would have been a thorn in Israel's flesh. Pharaoh did for Israel what they had failed to do for themselves.

This Pharaoh would have been Thutmosis I, who is known to have marched north on a military campaign that took him as far as the Euphrates River. He would have attacked Gezer on his way north. There is a thick layer of ash at Gezer that testifies to the accuracy of this record.

▼ *Famous bust of Queen Nefertiti.*

ROYAL WEDDING

To Solomon's bride David gave some very logical advice. "Listen, O daughter, consider and incline your ear; forget your own people also, and your father's house" (Ps. 45:10). If someone chooses to migrate to another country and culture, it is more conducive to happiness to identify with the new culture. With much admiration for her beauty he wrote, "The royal daughter is all glorious within the palace; her clothing is woven with gold. She shall be brought to the King in robes of many colors" (Ps. 45:13–14).

On his own behalf, Solomon wrote a superb wedding song to be sung responsively by himself, his bride, and a chorus of singers. The bride is called "Shulamite" (Song of Sol. 6:18), which is the feminine of "Shelomoh" — Solomon. In other words, Mrs. Solomon. She sang, "I am dark, but lovely, O daughters of Jerusalem" (Song of Sol. 1:5). Solomon responded by singing, "I have compared you, my love, to my filly among Pharaoh's chariots" (Song of Sol. 1:9).

Most brides today would not consider that as much of a compliment, but to Pharaoh's daughter it would have been regarded as the ultimate in compliments.

It should have been the beginning of married bliss, but unfortunately it did not last long. Moses had admonished Israel that if they set a king over themselves, he was not to "multiply horses for himself. . . . Neither shall he multiply wives for himself, lest his heart turn away" (Deut. 17:16–17). Solomon ignored this advice. "Solomon had forty thousand stalls of horses for his chariots, and twelve thousand horsemen" (1

▲ Statue of Pharaoh Hatshepsut, a name that means "Foremost of noble ladies."

▲ Expedition to Punt fresco in Mortual Temple of Hatshepsut.

Kings 4:26). On the matrimonial front, "He had seven hundred wives, princesses, and three hundred concubines" (1 Kings 11:3).

Critics may have questioned the feasibility of this record, but not long after Solomon, Pharaoh Amenhotep III came to the throne of Egypt, and he finished up with more than a thousand wives in his harem.

SOLOMON'S KINGDOM

"Solomon reigned over all kingdoms from the River [Euphrates] to the land of the Philistines, as far as the border of Egypt. They brought tribute and served Solomon all the days of his life" (1 Kings 4:21). His kingdom extended as far as "Tadmor in the wilderness" (1 Kings 9:18). In Roman times, Tadmor was known as Palmyra and was a very important oasis strategically located on the trade routes.

The opulence of Solomon's kingdom was breathtaking. "The king made silver as common in Jerusalem as stones" (1 Kings 10:27). He "built a fleet of ships at Ezion Geber. . . . And they went to Ophir, and acquired four hundred and twenty talents of gold" (1 Kings 9:26–28). Fourteen tons of gold!

Most Israeli archaeologists dismiss this record as historically unreliable. They have dated the reigns of David and Solomon to the early Iron Age II, and admittedly there is no evidence of affluence in that period. In fact, "poverty" would be a better word. So they question the very existence of David and Solomon, or suggest if they did exist it was only as minor tribal chiefs.

Finkelstein and Silberman in their book *David and Solomon* wrote, "The grandiose descriptions of Solomonic wealth and unchallenged royal power are absurdly discordant with the historical reality of the small, out-of-the-way hill country kingdom that possessed no literacy, no massive construction works, no extensive administration, and not the slightest sign of commercial prosperity."[1]

But here again they admit, "The biblical narrative is filled with so many specific details about trade transactions, monetary values, and complex royal administration that its authors seem to be describing a reality they knew from personal experience."[2]

However, a revised chronology would place the reigns of these kings in the Middle Bronze II period, and at that time there is abundant evidence of power and prosperity. Concerning this period, Dr. Amihai Mazar of the Hebrew University, in his book *Archaeology of the Land of the Bible*, wrote, "The second half of MBII was one of the most prosperous periods in the history of this culture, perhaps even its zenith."[3]

He also wrote, "The fortification systems of MBII reflect a period of great wealth and strong self-government in Syria and Palestine." And, "The Middle Bronze Age architecture was to a large extent innovative and original. Together with the massive fortifications of this period, it evidences a thriving, prosperous urban culture. The magnitude of the palaces and temples manifests the wealth and power concentrated in the hands of the autocracy and theocracy of the period."[4]

In his book *The Archaeology of the Israelite Settlement*, Israel Finkelstein wrote, "The entire country flourished in MB IIB. . . . In contrast to the extraordinary prosperity of MB II, the Late Bronze period was characterized by a severe crisis in settlement."[5] He also wrote, "In the Middle Bronze Age, six or seven centuries before the estimated time of David, massive walls and towers of an impressive city

1.   Israel Finkelstein and Neil Asher Silberman, *David and Solomon* (New York: Free Press, 2006), p. 153.
2.   Ibid., p. 153.
3.   Amihai Mazar, *Archaeology of the Land of the Bible 10,000–586 B.C.E.* (New York: Doubleday, 1990), p. 174.
4.   Ibid., p. 208, 214.
5.   Israel Finkelstein, *The Archaeology of the Israelite Settlement* (Jerusalem: Israel Exploration Society, 1988), p. 339.

◀ *Amenhotep I and wife, Ahmose-Meritamon.*

▼ *One of the large Osirid statues of Queen Hatshepsut in Luxor Egypt.*

fortification were built on the eastern slope of the city of David."[6]

Traditional archaeology would identify this MBII period as a continuation of the Canaanite period, but why would there be this sudden surge in affluence and power? It is more reasonable to recognize it as the time of Solomon.

SOLOMON'S WISDOM

Solomon was especially endowed with wisdom. An ingenious bit of psychology enabled him to make one critical decision. The incident is recorded in 1 Kings 3:16–27.

> Two women who were harlots came to the king, and stood before him. And one woman said, "O my lord, this woman and I dwell in the same house, and I gave birth while she was in the house. Then it happened, the third day after I had given birth, that this woman also gave birth. And we were together; no one was with us in the house, except the two of us in the house. And this woman's son died in the night, because she lay on him. So she arose in the middle of the night and took my son

from my side, while your handmaiden slept, and laid him in her bosom, and laid her dead child in my bosom. And when I rose in the morning to nurse my son, there he was, dead. But when I had examined him in the morning, indeed, he was not my son whom I had borne."

> Then the other woman said, "No! But the living one is my son, and the dead one is your son."

> And the first woman said, "No! But the dead one is your son, and the living one is my son." Thus they spoke before the king.

> And the king said, "The one says, 'This is my son, who lives, and your son is the dead one'; and the other says, 'No! But your son is the dead one, and my son is the living one.'" Then the king said, "Bring me a sword." So they brought a sword before the king. And the king said, "Divide the living child in two, and give half to one, and half to the other."

> Then the woman whose son was living spoke to the king, for she yearned with compassion for her son; and she said, "O my lord, give her the living child, and by no means kill him." But the other

6. Ibid., p. 274.

said, "Let him be neither mine nor yours, but divide him."

So the king answered and said, "Give the first woman the living child and by no means kill him; she is his mother."

Perhaps Solomon's greatest achievement was the building of the magnificent temple in Jerusalem. In this connection some very specific chronological information is given in 1 Kings 6:1, which enables us to calculate the date of the Exodus: "In the four hundred and eightieth year after the children of Israel had come out of the land of Egypt, in the fourth year of Solomon's reign over Israel, in the month of Ziv, which is the second month, that he began to build the house of the Lord." (See Appendix 2.)

Solomon came to the throne about 970 B.C. His fourth year would have been 966 B.C. The 480th year before that would be 1445 B.C., the biblical date for the Exodus.

THE QUEEN OF SHEBA

Another story that has fueled a lot of speculation is the visit of the Queen of Sheba to Solomon recorded in 1 Kings

10:1–2. "Now when the Queen of Sheba heard of the fame of Solomon concerning the name of the Lord, she came to test him with hard questions. She came to Jerusalem with a very great retinue, with camels that bore spices, very much gold, and precious stones." Much gold all right — four tons of it (1 Kings 10:10).

She is usually identified as coming from Yemen in Arabia, but this idea is based on some rather devious reasoning. It starts with Ketura, the last wife of Abraham, whose grandsons were Sheba and Dedan (Gen. 25:1–3). Isaiah 21:13 links the Dedanim with Arabia, so the assumption is that Sheba also went to Arabia, hence the Queen of Sheba came from Arabia.

Actually, the Hebrew text in 1 Kings 10:1 does not say "the Queen of Sheba" but simply "Queen Sheba." That seems to be her name rather than where she came from. But even supposing this queen did come from a place called Sheba, there was more than one Sheba. Cush was the progenitor of the Nubians south of Egypt (Gen. 10:7), and he had a grandson named Sheba. So Sheba could be south of Egypt.

However, we do not need to depend on such reasoning. Josephus wrote, "There was then a woman, queen of Egypt

▲ *The death mask of King Tutankhamun.*

▲ *Hatshepsut's Temple at Deir el Bahri, on the west bank of the Nile at Luxor, is set against the magnificent backdrop of the towering hills.*

and Ethiopia. . . . When this queen heard of the virtue and prudence of Solomon, she had a great mind to see him. . . . Accordingly, she came to Jerusalem with great splendour and rich furniture."[7] So Josephus identifies her, not with Arabia, but with Egypt and Ethiopia. The original word for Ethiopia is *Cush,* referring to Nubia, not the Ethiopia in East Africa.

And Jesus Christ called her the Queen of the South. In Daniel 11:8–9, the king of the south is identified as the king of Egypt, so the queen of the south would be the queen of Egypt, and by the revised chronology, that would be Queen Hatshepsut. That would mean we have the record from both ends — Solomon telling about the queen of Sheba coming to visit him, and on the walls of her temple at Luxor this queen tells of her visit to the land of Punt, taking many expensive gifts with her and returning loaded with gifts from the land she visited.

It is quite plausible that Hatshepsut could turn up with four tons of gold. Tutankhamen's tomb was loaded with gold. There was no shortage of it in Egypt, but it was not likely that an Arabian queen could have access to such a huge quantity of gold, much less bestow that much on Solomon.

Archaeologists are not agreed as to the location of Punt. Most say it is in east Africa, but there are a number of Egyptian inscriptions that link it with Lebanon, giving credence to the conclusion that the land of Punt was Israel, which, incidentally, Hatshepsut calls "God's Land."

That would suggest another reason for this remarkable excursion — Hatshepsut would be renewing acquaintance with her sister Neferbity, who was Solomon's wife. That could also explain how the queen of Sheba "heard of the fame of Solomon concerning the name of the Lord" (1 Kings 10:1). Her sister, who may have adopted Judaism as her religion, would have been in communication with her and told her about the religion of the LORD (Yehovah).

7.   Flavius Josephus, *Antiquities of the Jews*, Book VIII, chapter VI, para. 5.

Solomon no doubt inherited musical ability from his father David. "He spoke three thousand proverbs, and his songs were one thousand and five" (1 Kings 4:32). There are only 1,137 verses in the Book of Proverbs, so he must have spoken many others that are not recorded. The same applies to his songs. The Song of Solomon is made up of songs for his wedding ceremony, and he wrote two songs that are recorded in the Book of Psalms — 118, sung at the dedication of the temple, and 127, sung at the dedication of his palace. The remainder of his songs have not been left on record.

SOLOMON'S APOSTASY

But his forbidden wives were his downfall. It is hard to believe that such a wise man, so favored by God, could lapse into such depravity, but it happened. Of course it did not happen suddenly. It was just pernicious influences working insidiously over the years that resulted in disgraceful apostasy without Solomon realizing where it was leading him.

"And he had seven hundred wives, princesses, and three hundred concubines; and his wives turned away his heart. For it was so, when Solomon was old, that his wives turned his heart after other gods; and his heart was not loyal to the Lord his God, as was the heart of his father David" (1 Kings 11:3–4). He went so far as to build places of worship for these heathen deities on the Mount of Olives (1 Kings 11:7).

But there was a day of reckoning. "Therefore the Lord said to Solomon, 'Because you have done this, and have not kept My covenant and My statutes, which I have commanded you, I will surely tear the kingdom away from you and give it to your servant" (1 Kings 11:11). He would be allowed to keep the tribes of Judah and Benjamin, but the other ten tribes were to be given to his servant Jeroboam.

Solomon got the message. He repented of his shocking behavior and left on record in the Book of Ecclesiastes the

▲ *The citadel constructed by the Crusaders on Pharaoh's Island*

conclusions he drew from his wasted years, warning others not to follow in his foolish steps. "The words of the preacher, the son of David, king in Jerusalem. 'Vanity of vanities,' says the Preacher" (Eccles. 1:1–2). "I looked on all the works that my hands had done and on the labor in which I had toiled; and indeed all was vanity and grasping for the wind" (Eccles. 2:11).

He could not undo all the evil he had done. He could only admonish the new generation. "Remember now your Creator in the days of your youth. . . . Fear God and keep His commandments, for this is man's all" (Eccles. 12:1–13).

EZION-GEBER

There is one more record of Solomon's achievements that is of interest. "King Solomon also built a fleet of ships at Ezion-Geber, which is near Elath on the shore of the Red Sea" (1 Kings 9:26). Modern Eilat in Israel is at the head of the Gulf of Aqaba and is undoubtedly the "Elath on the shore of the Red Sea." It was assumed that Ezion-Geber must have been on the mainland near Elath, but in 1967 Alexander Flinder was scuba diving in the Red Sea seven and a half miles (12 km) south of Eilat. There is an island offshore called Jezirat Faraun (Pharaoh's Island), and he noted that while the water to the east of the island could be very turbulent, the water between the island and the Israeli shoreline seemed to be always very calm. He thought it

THE PEACE OF SOLOMON

Solomon "ruled over all the kingdoms west of the Euphrates River from Tiphsah to Gaza; he was at peace with all his neighbors" (1 Kings 4:24).

would be a good place for a harbor, but he thought no further about it till 1990 when it occurred to him that this may have been where Solomon's ships were kept.

There is archaeological evidence on the island for occupation as far back as the time of Solomon. On the west side is a small harbor that could have enabled a ship to shelter there, and of unusual interest is the fact that in Hebrew, *Ezion* means "backbone" and *Geber* means "man." The shape of the island gives the impression of a man lying face down in the water with his spine and the back of his head protruding from the water.

So Flinder, a pioneer in underwater archaeology in Britain, went back to Pharaoh's Island to explore not only its underwater features but its surface as well, and he concluded that this was indeed where Solomon's fleet sailed from.

THE KINGDOM DIVIDED

The Revolt ▲   ▲ Elijah Stands for God

Chapter 14

ISRAEL AND JUDAH

When Solomon died his kingdom was divided between his son Rehoboam, who reigned over Judah and Benjamin, and Jeroboam who reigned over the other ten tribes who became known as the kingdom of Israel. To discourage his people from going to Jerusalem to worship Jeroboam erected golden calves at Bethel and Dan for his people to worship. At Ashkelon Lawrence Stager found a silver calf that had been worshiped. In the fifth year of Rehoboam Shishak of Egypt occupied Jerusalem and took all the temple treasures back to Egypt. Shishak should probably be identified with Pharaoh Thutmosis III. Rehoboam was followed by Abijam and Asa who gained a great military victory at Mareshah. Jehoshaphat succeeded Asa. Jereboam was followed by a series of bad kings, the worst of whom was Ahab whose queen was Jezebel, a Phoenician princess who promoted the worship of Baal. The name of Jezebel has been found on a seal. The prophet Elijah challenged the priests of Baal to a contest on Mount Carmel. God answered Elijah's prayer and consumed his sacrifice. All the priests of Baal were slain.

Statue of the prophet Elijah at Muhraka on Mount Carmel.

AT THE DEATH OF SOLOMON HIS SON REHOBOAM came to the throne, and all Israel assembled at Shechem to anoint him as king. But first they wanted some assurance from Rehoboam that he would lighten the tax burdens Solomon had imposed on them to sustain his lavish lifestyle. At the advice of his young comrades, Rehoboam threatened to make their burdens even heavier.

It was a rash decision and he paid the price. Jeroboam, who had served under Solomon, led a revolt and ten tribes united under him to make a separate state known as Israel. Rehoboam was left with the two tribes of Judah and Benjamin in the south.

Jeroboam feared that if his subjects went to Jerusalem for the rites required of them at the temple they might be inclined to transfer their loyalty to Rehoboam, so he set up two centers of worship in Israel. "Therefore the king asked advice, made two calves of gold. . . . He set up one in Bethel, and the other he put in Dan," the south and north extremities of his kingdom (1 Kings 12:28–29).

These golden calves have never been found. They would have been melted down for their gold long ago, but when Lawrence Stager was excavating at Ashkelon he was surprised to find a small shrine at the north gate of the city, and inside was a silver-plated calf. Most of the silver was gone, but it confirms that calves had been worshiped in Israel.

EGYPTIAN CLUES

It happened in the fifth year of King Rehoboam, that Shishak king of Egypt came up against Jerusalem. And he took away the treasures of the house of the Lord and the treasures of the king's house; he took away everything. He also took away all the gold shields which Solomon had made (1 Kings 14:25–26).

This pharaoh is usually identified with the Sheshonq of Dynasty 22 who left a record on the south wall of the temple of Karnak of the cities he claims to have conquered, but Jerusalem is not among them. It is argued that some of the place names have been eroded away, but Jerusalem should have been at the top of the list. It is not there. In any case, this list is just a copy of other reliefs and it is apparent that it did not happen. It was just some Pharaonic boasting.

By the revised chronology, Shishak would be identified with Thutmosis III, who left the record of his conquests in the north. On the temple wall at Karnak is a list of the treasures he brought back from his conquests, and they correspond very well with the articles known to have been in Solomon's temple.

Solomon had made 300 shields of hammered gold (1 Kings 10:17), and 300 gold shields are depicted on the Karnak temple wall. Solomon's temple had two doors plated with gold (1 Kings 6:32), and on the Karnak wall are two gold-plated doors, and so the list goes on. The difference in the names of Shishak and Thutmosis is not significant. In foreign countries names were often totally different.

THE KINGS

Rehoboam was followed by his son Abijam, who ruled for only three years, and then came his son, the good King Asa, who ruled for 41 years. Asa was responsible

▲ *The remains of Ahab's palace in Samaria.*

▲ *The rubble of what was Ahab's place of rule.*

for a great religious revival. He got rid of the foreign gods that had been erected and cut down the wooden images. The land enjoyed ten years of peace, but then came trouble.

"Zerah the Ethiopian came out against them with an army of a million men and three hundred chariots, and he came to Mareshah" (2 Chron. 14:9). Asa's army was hopelessly outnumbered and Asa knew that, humanly speaking, he had no hope, but he had been faithful to God and he offered a simple but very beautiful prayer.

"Asa cried out to the Lord his God, and said, 'Lord, it is nothing for You to help, whether with many or with those who have no power; help us O Lord our God, for we rest on You and in Your name we go against this multitude. O Lord, you are our God; do not let man prevail against You!" (2 Chron. 14:11). His prayer was answered. "So the Lord struck the Ethiopians before Asa and Judah, and the Ethiopians fled" (verse 12).

I have often tried to visualize this dramatic scene. Mareshah was one of the most important cities in Israel in Old Testament times. It has been my privilege to take a group of volunteers to Mareshah for the last eight years where the Israeli Antiquities Authority has allocated us a site to excavate. I have often stood on top of the tell and looked southward toward Egypt, trying to picture this formidable army marching up the valley with their glittering chariots. Of course I do not know exactly where the conflict took place, but I like to imagine seeing it all happening.

Orthodox archaeologists have had some trouble trying to identify this Zerah the Ethiopian. Of course it was not the Ethiopia we are familiar with in East Africa. Ethiopia in the Bible refers to Kush, what we today call the Sudan. By the standard chronology, no such king is known, nor could anyone in Dynasty 22 raise such a formidable army, so the critics have written it off as unhistorical.

However, by the reduced chronology this would be

Amenhotep II, the son of Thutmosis III, who records two northern invasions. His capital was at Luxor, which is not far from the Sudan, so he could have been called an Ethiopian by the Bible writer. He does not record a defeat, but it is significant that he does little boasting about his victories. That is out of character for a pharaoh who has won a battle.

Asa was followed by his son Jehoshaphat, who was also a good king, but the same cannot be said about the kings who followed Jereboam in Israel. Some were bad and the others were worse. Ahab was the worst of them all, mainly because he married the strong-minded Phoenician princess Jezebel. Ahab's father, Omri, had purchased a hill from a man called Shemer, and he built a city on it called Samaria. It became the capital city of Israel.

CONFRONTING AHAB

Ahab built a temple for Baal in Samaria and "went and served Baal and worshiped him" (1 Kings 16:31). Baal was supposed to be the weather god, the god who sent rain and fertility for the crops, but there was a young man in Gilead who was praying that there would be no rain to refresh the crops. "Elijah was a man with a nature like ours, and he prayed earnestly that it would not rain" (James 5:17).

God not only answered his prayer, He commissioned Elijah to confront the king of Israel. Striding past the palace guards, he confronted the astonished king with the startling message, " 'As the Lord God of Israel lives, before whom I stand, there shall not be dew nor rain these years, except at my word' " (1 Kings 17:1). Before the king could recover his senses, Elijah turned on his heel and strode out of the palace.

It was not long before the parched earth testified to the veracity of the prophet's words, and Ahab blamed Elijah for his plight. He searched everywhere, even sending to foreign countries to apprehend the prophet whom he held responsible for his country's blistering drought, but Elijah had

◀ *Ruins at the site of Ugarit where tablets were found detailing the worship of Baal.*

answer them but nothing happened. Elijah taunted them with their inability to get results. " 'Cry aloud,' " he said, " 'for he is a god; either he is meditating, or he is busy, or he is on a journey, or perhaps he is sleeping and must be awakened' " (1 Kings 18:27).

DETAILS SUPPORTED

This challenge was not without meaning. In 1929 archaeologists found Ugarit in Syria. On the summit of the tell they uncovered a temple to Baal. Also in the library of the chief priest of Baal they found 15 cuneiform tablets that revealed much about the worship of Baal.

Michael Coogan wrote a fascinating book called *Stories from Ancient Canaan* in which he quotes from these tablets. "Baal will begin the rainy season, the season of wadis in flood; and he will sound his voice in the clouds, flash his lightning to the earth."[1] Baal was indeed the storm god, but he was the type of god who went on holidays, got sick, and even died. "Baal the conqueror has died. The Prince, the Lord of the earth has perished."[2]

But he recovered. "Baal the conqueror lives, the Prince, the Lord of the earth, has revived. The heavens poured down oil, the wadis ran with honey."[3] In the meantime, prayers to Baal would have to be put on hold. Elijah taunted them with this possibility.

One of the poems relates how El, a subordinate god, afflicted himself before Baal. "He cut his skin with a knife, he made incisions with a razor, he cut his cheeks and skin, he raked his arms with a reed, he plowed his chest like a garden, he raked his back like a valley."[4]

taken refuge in Phoenicia, of all places, the country from which Jezebel and the religion of Baal had come.

Three and a half years later, Elijah went to meet King Ahab again and demanded that he gather all Israel together on Mount Carmel. That was a real challenge because Mount Carmel was regarded as sacred to Baal worshipers. The monarch meekly obeyed and the contest began.

Elijah proposed that the prophets of Baal offer a sacrificial bull on an altar and call down fire to consume it. The prophets of Baal could hardly object. Baal was supposed to be the deity who controlled thunder, lightning, and rain.

For six hours the false prophets pleaded with Baal to

That gives meaning to the Bible record that said that in their desperation, "They cried aloud, and cut themselves, as was their custom, with knives and lances, until the blood gushed out on them" (1 Kings 18:28).

There is just one problem with this synchronism between Ugarit and Elijah — the traditional chronology would place the Ugarit tablets more than 400 years before the time of Elijah, making a comparison irrelevant. By a

1.   Michael Coogan, *Stories from Ancient Canaan* (Philadelphia, PA: Westminster Press, 1978), p. 79.
2.   Ibid., p. 110.
3.   Ibid., p. 113.
4.   Ibid., p. 109.

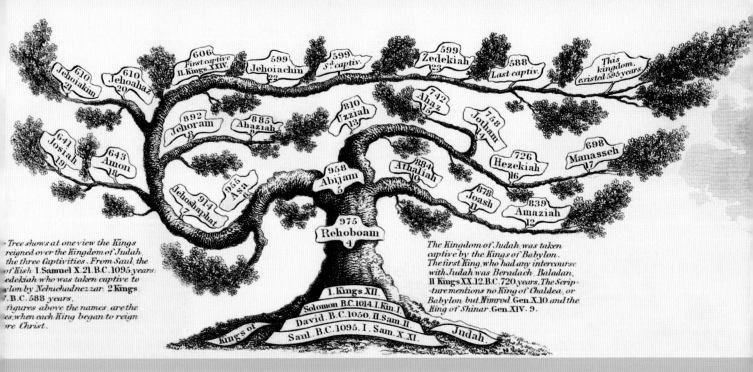

The figures above the names are the dates B.C. when each King began to reign. Tree shows at one view the Kings who reigned over the Kingdom of Judah, the three Captivities. From Saul, the son of Kish 1.Samuel X.21.B.C.1095 years, to Zedekiah who was taken captive to Babylon by Nebuchadnezzar. 2 Kings XXV. B.C.588 years.

The Kingdom of Judah, was taken captive by the Kings of Babylon. The first King who had any intercourse with Judah was Beradach, Baladan, II Kings XX.12.B.C.720 years.The Scriptures mentions no King of Chaldea, or Babylon but Nimrod Gen.X.10.and the King of Shinar. Gen.XIV. 9.

▲ *The Rehoboam family tree from Leonard's Chronological Chart of History.*

reduced chronology, as advocated in this book, the cultures would be contemporary.

But Baal turned a deaf ear and finally the false prophets sullenly withdrew from the contest. Then Elijah offered his sacrifice. " 'Fill four water pots with water, and pour it on the burnt sacrifice and on the wood.' Then he said, 'Do it a second time.' " He wanted to demonstrate there was no trickery being practiced (1 Kings 18:33–34).

Water on top of Mount Carmel in a drought? Where would all that water come from?

It cannot be proved where all this took place. Mount Carmel is a long ridge of mountains extending 19 miles (30 km) from Haifa to Jezreel. We can only conclude it was within sight of the Mediterranean and somewhere where water was available. There is only one such known site, and a church to memorialize Elijah has been built on the spot. Just below the church is a well. But how water can be available in a well on top of a mountain is hard to say.

Elijah offered a simple prayer and lightning flashed from heaven, consuming the sacrifice and the altar. The multitudes were obliged to confess, " 'The LORD [Yehovah], He is God! The Lord, He is God!' " (1 Kings 18:39). Elijah then slew all the prophets of Baal.

When Jezebel heard this she was furious and threatened Elijah with death. Incredibly, this great man of God was intimidated by a woman and fled to Mount Sinai.

A QUEEN'S SEAL?

Jezebel was no fictitious figure. In 1964 Nahman Avigad purchased a seal on the antiquities market and announced that he thought it might be the seal of Queen Jezebel, but there is always a doubt about artifacts that turn up on the antiquities market. Now some modern scholarship has been applied to it that may confirm the nature of the seal. Marjo Korpel, a Dutch researcher, has put in some intense study on the seal. She concludes that it is genuine and does have the name of Jezebel on it. She says she feels 99 percent sure that it is genuine.

The readable letters on the seal are YZBL. The *Y* at the beginning is no problem as there is no *J* in the Hebrew alphabet. Wherever you read a name beginning with *J* in the English Bible you can substitute *Y* for *J*. Jerusalem should really begin with a *Y* and Jezebel's name was really Yezebel. There were also no vowels in the old Hebrew alphabet so YZBL could be read *Jezebel*.

There is one other problem, however. In the Hebrew Bible, Jezebel's name is prefaced with the Hebrew letter *aleph*, the first letter of the alphabet. From it the Greek letter *alpha* came and the English word "alphabet." *Aleph* was not actually a letter. It rather signified that a vowel went there, but there is no *aleph* on the Jezebel seal.

This is where Korpel's speculation comes in. There are indications at the top of the seal that there were two letters there, and she claims that one of the missing letters at the top of the seal could have been the missing *aleph*.

The Bible says that Jezebel "wrote letters in Ahab's name, sealed them with his seal," but no doubt she also had her own seal.

EMPIRES CLASH

Ahab's Death ▲   Nineveh

Chapter 15

ISRAEL AND ASSYRIA

After Ahab's death Moab revolted against Israel but Jehoram and Jehoshaphat defeated the Moabites, an incident is also recorded on the Moabite stone found in Jordan. By traditional chronology the Hittite empire ended about 1,200 BC but here they were in the ninth century BC; further support for a reduced chronology. When Jehu became king of Israel he was obliged to pay tribute to the Assyrian king Shalmaneser III. The Shalmeneser obelisk in the British Museum depicts Jehu kneeling before Shalmaneser and offering him tribute. God commissioned Jonah to warn the Assyrians in Nineveh that God would destroy the city. The whole city repented and Nineveh was spared. This incident would have occurred under Adad Nirari III who left a record of a religious revival that took place during his reign. In 722 BC the Assyrians conquered Samaria and sent most of the population into exile. They were replaced by Assyrian settlers who became known as the Samaritans.

ISRAEL HAD PROSPERED UNDER THE REIGN OF AHAB, and Moab had been obliged to pay tribute to Israel, but when Ahab was killed in battle and his son Ahaziah mounted the throne, Moab seized the opportunity to rebel. "Mesha king of Moab was a sheepbreeder, and he regularly paid the king of Israel one hundred thousand lambs and the wool of one hundred thousand rams. But it happened, when Ahab died, that the king of Moab rebelled against the king of Israel" (2 Kings 3:4–5).

Ahaziah ruled for only two years, then his brother Jehoram took the throne. He raised an army and took to the field against Mesha. He also persuaded Jehoshaphat, the king of Judah, to join him in the assault on Moab. The coalition defeated the Moabite army in the field and caused a lot of havoc in the land, but they were not able to conquer Mesha's city Kir Hareseth, probably the present-day city of Kerak where there is an impressive Crusader castle.

This record has been preserved in the Bible, and Mesha also left a record of the incident. In 1868 F. Klein, a German missionary, visited Diban in Jordan where he saw a black stone with some Hebrew writing on it. The local Arabs had no idea of its importance, but when they saw Klein's interest in the stone they demanded a high price for its purchase.

Klein hurried back to Jerusalem and thence to Germany to raise the money, but in the meantime Charles Clermont-Ganneau, a French scholar, heard of the discovery and hurried to the site. With difficulty, he persuaded the Arabs to allow him to make a squeeze of the writing, and on his return persuaded the French government to allocate the money for its purchase.

However, when he returned, the stone was missing. The Arabs had lit a fire over the stone, then poured cold water on it, breaking it up into many pieces, and they had distributed the pieces among themselves. He was only able to recover about one-third of the original stone, but with the help of the squeeze it was possible to reconstruct the full stone, which is now in the Louvre in Paris.

The inscription said, "I am Mesha, son of Chemosh, king of Moab . . . Omri [Ahab's father] was king of Israel and oppressed Moab many days, for Chemosh was angry with his land. And his son succeeded him and he also said, I will oppress Moab. In my days he said this, but I got the upper hand of him and his house."

Sometime after this the Syrians besieged Samaria, causing a severe famine in the city. The inhabitants became so desperate for food that four lepers decided to cast themselves on the mercy of the Syrians, reasoning that they were going to die of starvation anyway so they had nothing to lose if the Syrians killed them.

▼ *Sculptured tablet of Tiglath Pileser III, who led the Assyrian Empire.*

On reaching the camp they were astonished to find no one there, "For the Lord had caused the army of the Syrians to hear the noise of chariots and the noise of horses — the noise of a great army; so they said one to another, 'Look, the king of Israel has hired against us the kings of the Hittites and the kings of the Egyptians to attack us.' Therefore they arose and fled" (2 Kings 7:6–7).

Now there is something terribly wrong here. According to the traditional pundits, the Hittites came to their end about 1200 B.C.,

▲ *Assyrian relief, showing the brutality of men being skinned alive.*

▲ *Assyrian relief of men being impaled, very likely the beginnings of what became crucifixion.*

but here they are in the ninth century B.C., not just in existence but named ahead of the mighty Egyptian Empire. Another biblical blunder?

If this was the only reference to the Hittites at this time some might be tempted to think so, but it so happens that the Assyrian records also tell of their wars against the Hittites. In the ninth century B.C. Shalmaneser III told of his all-out wars against the Hittites, and in the eighth century B.C. Sennacherib was also at war with them. How do the traditionalists wriggle out of this one, especially as the names of the Hittite kings mentioned in the Assyrian accounts are the same as the Hittite kings before 1200 B.C.?

O.R. Gurney, in his book *The Hittites*, says, "In the south-eastern provinces of the Hittite Empire Hittite culture had a strange afterglow which lasted for no less than five centuries. Assyrian records continue to refer to Syria and the Taurus area as the 'Land of Hatti' and speak of kings bearing names like Sapalulme, Mutallu, Katuzili, and Labarna (cf. Suppiluliumas, Muwatallis, Hattusilis or Kantuzzilis, Labarnas)."[1]

A strange afterglow! An interesting expression, but it does not explain anything.

So it is the same old story. The time of the Hittite demise is based on synchronisms with Egypt and they are demonstrably inflated. The Assyrian records are much more reliable and are consistent with the Bible chronology. The Bible was right in putting the Hittites ahead of the Egyptians. Rameses II fought the Battle of Kadesh against the Hittites and was lucky to escape with his life.

ASSYRIAN CONNECTIONS

Jehu, an army officer under Jehoram, was the next to seize the throne of Israel. Anointed a king under Elisha's direction, he set out in his chariot for Jezreel. Observers saw him

coming and reported to the king that he drove furiously. A real speedster. He caught up with Jehoram and shot an arrow through his heart (2 Kings 9:24).

Henry Layard found a large obelisk in his excavations at Nimrud in Assyria. One of the panels shows Jehu prostrate before the Assyrian king, presenting tribute to him. This obelisk is now in the British Museum. There is close agreement between the chronologies of Assyria and Israel.

There are three books in the Bible that deal with the Assyrians. First is the epic story of Jonah and the whale, strictly speaking "a great fish," which the Lord had prepared to swallow Jonah (Jonah 1:17). Most whales have small throats unable to swallow anything as large as a man, but there is a known incident when this happened. It was reported in several newspapers. We quote from the *Indian Sunday Statesman*, May 25, 1953:

> One of the most miraculous escapes from death and an experience almost unique in world history befell a seaman named James Bartley one February day in 1891.
>
> Bartley was a seaman on the American whaler *Star of the East*. On this particular day the *Star of the East* was battling against a storm in the Antarctic Sea. Then the look-out man spotted a whale, and despite the rough weather all the hands were quickly at work. Soon the deadly harpoon found its mark.
>
> Then followed the inevitable "battle" with the great creature which dived deeply and twisted and turned to throw off the "stinging thing" in its back.
>
> As suddenly as it started the struggle ended, and the crew saw that their catch was indeed a mighty sperm whale. The engines were stopped and the boats were lowered to bring the whale to the ship's side.
>
> In one of the boats was James Bartley, an

1.   O.R. Gurney, *The Hittites* (London; Baltimore, MD: Penguin Books, 1952), p. 39.

▲ *An interior room in the Kerak Castle, located in Kerak in Jordan. It is one of the largest crusader castles in the Levant. (Inset) Exterior view of the castle.*

experienced sailor. Approaching the creature's tail Bartley was about to attach his coiled rope to it when the whale shivered. Its tail flashed and in a split second Bartley's boat had been flung high into the air. Both he and his mates were tossed into the boiling seas.

The sudden and unexpected return to life of the whale took all by surprise, for it had seemed quite dead. But such things had happened before and the whaler's mate was already standing on the deck with his rifle at the ready. Two shots cracked out as he fired and the whale, hit in a vital spot, reared up from the water, opened its mighty jaws in the last quiver of death, then momentarily disappeared beneath the churning waters.

In seconds it reappeared, quite dead. Then the skipper remembered Bartley. The second boat was ordered to search for the two men but there was no sign of them. Giving them up as dead, the skipper had the whale roped and hauled aboard, then began the laborious task of cutting it up. Unexpectedly, one of the men on this job let out a cry and began to hack furiously at the belly of the creature.

"There's something there — in its belly," he shouted. "Help me quickly."

Others hastened to help and there before their amazed eyes was the unconscious figure of James Bartley. Stripped, massaged and swathed in blankets in a warm cabin Bartley soon recovered to tell his tale to his awestruck mates.

None of this proves that Jonah was really swallowed by a whale, a shark, or some other big fish. It simply shows that a whale could swallow a man. Of course the Book of Jonah is more the story of Jonah and Nineveh. Jonah prophesied during the reign of Jeroboam, the son of Joash, who ruled from 793 to 753 B.C. He was told to go to Nineveh and "cry out against it; for their wickedness" (Jon. 1:2).

Jonah had no doubt heard about what the Assyrians did to people they did not like, and he figured that the sort of message he was commissioned to proclaim would not be a very popular message. He would probably finish up by being impaled or skinned alive. Not relishing such a prospect he took off in the opposite direction and paid his passage at Joppa (now a suburb of Tel Aviv) on a boat that was headed for Tarshish in Spain.

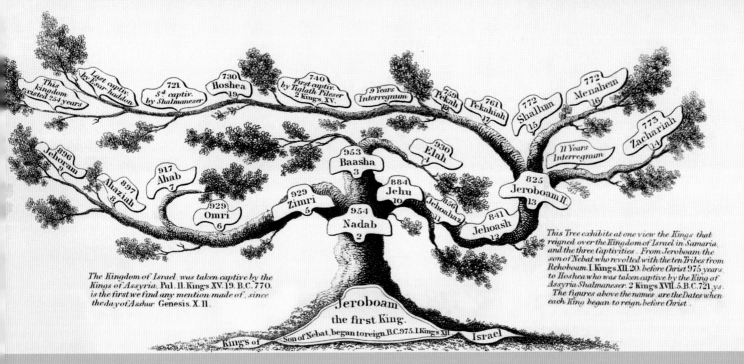

The labels on the tree read:

- This kingdom existed 254 years
- Last captiv: by Esar haddon
- 721 3d captiv. by Shalmaneser.
- 730 Hoshea 19
- 740 First captiv. by Tiglath Pileser 2 Kings. XV.
- 9 Years Interregnum
- 759 Pekah 18
- 761 Pekahiah 17
- 772 Shallum 15
- 772 Menahem 16
- 773 Zachariah 14
- 11 Years Interregnum
- 896 Jehoram 9
- 917 Ahab 7
- 953 Baasha 3
- 930 Elah 4
- 897 Ahaziah 8
- 929 Omri 6
- 929 Zimri 5
- 884 Jehu 10
- 856 Jehoahaz 11
- 825 Jeroboam II 13
- 841 Jehoash 12
- 954 Nadab 2

The Kingdom of Israel, was taken captive by the Kings of Assyria. Pul. II.Kings XV.19. B.C.770. is the first we find any mention made of, since the day of Asshur. Genesis. X.11.

This Tree exhibits at one view the Kings that reigned over the Kingdom of Israel in Samaria, and the three Captivities. From Jeroboam the son of Nebat who revolted with the ten Tribes from Rehoboam. I.Kings XII.20. before Christ 975 years, to Hoshea who was taken captive by the King of Assyria Shalmaneser. 2 Kings XVII.5.B.C.721 ys. The figures above the names, are the Dates when each King began to reign, before Christ.

Jeroboam the first King. Son of Nebat, began to reign B.C.975. I.Kings XII

King's of Israel

▲ *The family tree of Jeroboam from Leonard's Chronological Chart of History (see page 110).*

NINEVEH AND SHALMANESER

It was on this journey that a tempestuous storm arose and Jonah was flung into the sea and swallowed by this big fish. When the fish spat him out on the Phoenician beach (there is a beach in Lebanon today fronting water called Jonah's Bay), it was then that Jonah decided to go quietly and set out for Nineveh, the capital of Assyria.

To Jonah's surprise, "The people of Nineveh believed God, proclaimed a fast, and put on sackcloth, from the greatest to the least of them. Then word came to the king of Nineveh. . . . And he caused it to be proclaimed. . . . let every one turn from his evil way" (Jon. 3:5–8).

The Assyrian king at this time was Adad Nirari III, who ruled from 810 to 782 B.C. It so happens that a religious revival took place under this king. Whether it is the revival that came as the result of Jonah's preaching cannot be determined.

Jonah's name is not mentioned in the Assyrian record. All that can be said is that such a revival did take place around this time.

A series of bad kings in Israel terminated with Hoshea, who "did evil in the sight of the Lord. . . . Shalmaneser king of Assyria came up against him; and Hoshea became his vassal, and paid him tribute" (2 Kings 17:2–3). This would have been Shalmaneser V, who ruled from 732 to 722 B.C. But Hoshea stopped paying tribute and tried to enter into an alliance with So, king of Egypt.

By now Egypt was in decline and was no help to Israel. "Now the king of Assyria went throughout all the land, and went up to Samaria and besieged it for three years" (2 Kings 17:5). Just before Samaria fell to the Assyrians there was a palace coup and Sennacherib seized the throne.

Significantly, the Bible does not say that Shalmaneser captured Samaria, but "in the ninth year of Hoshea, the king of Assyria took Samaria and carried Israel away to Assyria" (2 Kings 17:6). That was in 722 B.C.

This left a vacuum in the depopulated land, so the king of Assyria replaced them with people from Babylon and Syria, "and they took possession of Samaria and dwelt in its cities" (2 Kings 17:24).

However, because of the depleted population, lions multiplied in the land "which killed some of them" (2 Kings 17:25). The people attributed this problem to their ignorance of the "rituals of the God of the land" (verse 26). So the Assyrian king rounded up some of the exiled Levites and sent priests to instruct them, but they still clung to their own gods and finished up with a religion in which "they feared the Lord, yet served their own gods" (verse 33).

They were called Samaritans (verse 29), some of whom still live in Nablus, near Samaria, today. They have their own ancient scroll of the Pentateuch that they carefully follow, even to killing a Passover lamb on Mount Gerizim. In Jesus' day they were despised by the Jews, though not by Jesus, who told the parable of the Good Samaritan.

HEZEKIAH'S HUMILIATION

Judah Conquered ▲   ▲ Nineveh's Doom

Chapter 16

JUDAH AND ASSYRIA

When Sennacherib first threatened Jerusalem Hezekiah bought him off with 300 talents of silver and 30 talents of gold. Assyrian cuneiform cylinders support this record. Following this incident the prophet Isaiah told Hezekiah he was going to die. Hezekiah prayed and 15 years were added to his life. As a token that it would happen, the sun went backwards ten degrees. The Babylonians observed this phenomenon and sent a delegation to Hezekiah to learn more about its cause. Hezekiah prepared for the return of the Assyrians by strengthening his army and digging a tunnel to bring the water from the spring Gihon into the city. When Sennacherib returned to Jerusalem an angel killed 185,000 Assyrian soldiers and Sennacherib returned to Nineveh. Later he was assassinated by two of his sons. Ashur-bani-pal was the last great king of Assyria. In 612 BC the combined armies of Babylon and Media conquered Nineveh and destroyed it.

SENNACHERIB THEN TURNED HIS ATTENTION TO Jerusalem, but that was a different story. Hezekiah was now king and "he did what was right in the sight of the LORD" (2 Kings 18:3). "And in the fourteenth year of King Hezekiah, Sennacherib king of Assyria came up against all the fortified cities of Judah and took them" (verse 13).

Sennacherib's record tells us how many cities of Judah he conquered. "As to Hezekiah the Jew, he did not submit to my yoke, I laid siege to 46 of his strong cities, walled forts, and to the countless small villages in their vicinity, and conquered them by means of well-stamped earth ramps, and battering rams brought thus near to the walls, combined with the attack by foot soldiers using mines, breaches as well as sapper work. I drove out (of them) 200,150 people, young and old, male and female, horses, mules, donkeys, camels, big and small cattle beyond counting, and considered them booty."[1]

At first Hezekiah's faith wavered. "Then Hezekiah king of Judah sent to the king of Assyria at Lachish saying, 'I have done wrong; turn away from me; whatever you impose on me I will pay.' And the king of Assyria assessed Hezekiah king of Judah three hundred talents of silver and thirty talents of gold" (2 Kings 18:14–15).

In the British Museum is a cuneiform cylinder that records this incident. "Himself I made a prisoner in Jerusalem his royal residence, like a bird in a cage. . . . Hezekiah himself, whom my terror-inspiring splendor of my lordship had overwhelmed and whose regular and elite troops which he had brought into Jerusalem his royal residence, in order to strengthen it, had deserted him, did send me later to Nineveh my lordly city, together with 30 talents of gold, 800 talents of silver, precious stones."[2]

You will notice a slight discrepancy in the amount of tribute of silver that was paid. The fault is not with the Bible. It was an Assyrian scribal error because there is a similar prism in the Chicago Museum that says 300 talents of silver.

HEZEKIAH'S REFORMATION

It was a humiliating submission by Hezekiah, but God taught him a valuable lesson. "In those days Hezekiah was sick and near death. And Isaiah the prophet, the son of Amoz, went to him and said to him, 'Thus says the Lord: "Set your house in order for you shall die and not live" ' " (2 Kings 20:1).

Hezekiah did not particularly want to die and "he turned his face toward the wall, and prayed to the Lord, saying 'Remember now, O Lord, I pray, how I have walked before You in truth and with a loyal heart, and have done what was good in Your sight" (2 Kings 20:2–3). It is still common practice for Jewish people today to pray facing a wall.

It was true. Hezekiah had brought about a great reformation in Judah, getting rid of all the pagan gods that had crept into the land, but it was not his good works that counted with God. Good works can never earn our salvation. God sent another

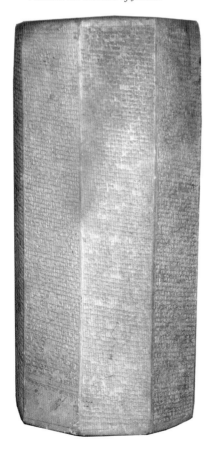

1. James Maxwell Miller and John Haralson Hayes, *A History of Ancient Israel and Judah* (Louisville, KY: Westminster John Knox Press, 2006), p. 361).
2. James Pritchard, *The Ancient Near East* (Princeton, NJ: Princeton University Press, 1958), p. 206–208.

▼ *The six-sided Sennacherib prism found at the site of ancient Ninevah recounts the invasion of Judah.*

▲ *A mosque on the site of the palace of Esarhadon at Nineveh.*

▲ *A portion of Hezekiah Tunnel, which is over 1,800 feet in length.*

message through Isaiah saying, " 'I have heard your prayer, I have seen your tears; surely I will heal you' " (2 Kings 20:5). It is genuine repentance that counts with God.

Hezekiah was healed and God added 15 years to his life, which Hezekiah made good use of. He knew Sennacherib would return, so he strengthened the fortifications of Jerusalem, and he "stopped the water outlet of Upper Gihon, and brought the water by tunnel to the west side of the city of David" (2 Chron. 32:30).

HEZEKIAH'S TUNNEL

This tunnel was a phenomenal achievement. I take a group to Egypt, Jordan, and Israel every year, and in Jerusalem I give them the opportunity of wading through Hezekiah's Tunnel. It is an experience they never forget.

The tunnel is over 1,800 feet (560 m) long and starts at the Gihon Spring. *Gihon* is a Hebrew word meaning "gushing," a very appropriate name because the water used to gush out every few minutes and then stop, only to repeat the process a little later.

There was an inscription on the wall near the end of the tunnel. It read, "This is the story of the boring through. While (the tunnelers lifted) the pick-axe each toward his fellow and while 3 cubits (remained yet) to be bored (through, there was heard) the voice of a man calling to his fellow — for there was a split (or overlap) in the rock on the right hand and on (the left hand). When the tunnel was driven through, the tunnelers hewed the rock, each man toward his fellow, pick-axe against pick-axe. And the water flowed from the spring toward the reservoir for 1200 cubits. The height of the rock above the head of the tunnelers was a hundred cubits."

Pick marks on the sides of the tunnel walls indicate that they did indeed start from both ends and meet in the middle. How they did so is a mystery because the tunnel does not go in a straight line. Why it took such a circuitous

course is not known. Several theories have been advanced but none of them can be proved.

SENNACHERIB RETURNS

As expected, Sennacherib returned. Lachish had been conquered and its citizens exiled to Assyria. Lachish was built on a steep hill with a strong wall around it, and Sennacherib was so pleased with his conquest that he had extensive reliefs carved onto the walls of his palace at Nineveh. Layard found these reliefs and sent them back to the British Museum where they are today.

"Then the king of Assyria sent the Tartan, the Rabsaris, and the Rabshakeh from Lachish, with a great army against Jerusalem" (2 Kings 18:17). Hezekiah knew he had no hope against the powerful Assyrian army and appealed to the prophet Isaiah for divine intervention. Isaiah sent him the comforting message that Sennacherib would "not come into this city, nor shoot an arrow there" (2 Kings 19:32).

"And it came to pass on a certain night that the angel of the Lord went out, and killed in the camp of the Assyrians one hundred and eighty five thousand. . . . So Sennacherib king of Assyria departed and went away, returned home, and remained at Nineveh. Now it came to pass, as he was worshiping in the temple of Nisroch his god, that his sons Adrammelech and Sharezer struck him down with the sword; and they escaped into the land of Ararat. Then Esarhaddon his son reigned in his place" (2 Kings 19:35–37).

Needless to say, the Assyrians did not see fit to leave a record of their humiliating retreat from Jerusalem, but Sennacherib did say on his prism, "Himself I made a prisoner in Jerusalem his royal residence, like a bird in a cage,"[3] which was an admission that though he had besieged Jerusalem, he had not conquered the city.

---

3.   E.A. Speiser and James B. Pritchard, *Ancient Near Eastern Texts Relating to the New Testament*, 3rd ed. (Princeton, NJ: Princeton University Press, 1969), p. 287–288.

▲ *Reproduction of the great gateway to the ancient city of Nineveh.*

History also confirms that his sons assassinated him and that Esarhaddon had followed him on the throne. Esarhaddon invaded Egypt but did not trouble Israel. He built a new palace for himself in Nineveh. Archaeologists have not been able to excavate this palace because Muslims have built a mosque on top of it. Within the mosque is a tomb claimed to be the tomb of Jonah the prophet.

THE DOOM OF NINEVEH

Ashurbanipal was the last great king of Assyria. He was very keen on hunting lions and left many reliefs of his exploits while lion hunting, but the Assyrians had recovered from their fears aroused by Jonah's startling message and their doom was sealed. This time there would be no reprieve.

The prophet Nahum wrote, "The burden against Nineveh. The book of the vision of Nahum the Elkoshite. . . . He will make an utter end of it. . . . The Lord has given a command concerning you: 'Your name shall be perpetuated no longer. . . . I will dig your grave, for you are vile' " (Nah. 1:1–14). Nineveh was to be buried and forgotten.

In 612 the combined armies of Babylon and Media conquered Nineveh and destroyed it. Nineveh was not rebuilt and the dust of time blew over it — 200 years later no one knew where Nineveh was. When Henry Layard excavated Nimrud he thought he had found Nineveh. He was wrong. It was not until he excavated Kuyunjik, on the east bank of the River Tigris opposite Mosul, that he found evidence that this was indeed Nineveh.

Zephaniah also predicted Nineveh's doom. "He will stretch out his hand against the north,

Ashurbanipal stele ▶

A relief from Nineveh showing Ashurbanipal driving a sword through a lion. ▶

destroy Assyria, and make Nineveh a desolation, as dry as the wilderness. The herds shall lie down in her midst" (Zeph. 2:13–14).

God had predicted that Babylon "will never be inhabited . . . nor will the Arabian pitch tents there, nor will the shepherds make their sheepfolds there" (Isa. 13:20). When I first visited Babylon in 1958, my family and I slept overnight among its ruins. We had Babylon to ourselves, and I noted that the ground seemed salty. There was no sign of pastures for sheep and there were no flocks there.

After Babylon we traveled north to Nineveh. I hoped against hope that I might see a shepherd with his flock among its ruins. I need not have worried. Nineveh is buried under rolling hills covered with verdure. There were flocks and herds everywhere among its ruins. When one young shepherdess saw me with my camera to my eye she abandoned her small flock and fled in terror. I later learned that people here believe that if they are photographed an enemy could stick a pin in the picture of a person and that person would then suffer a bodily wound.

So the prophets knew what they were talking about. Nineveh was buried and forgotten for some 2,500 years.

▲ *An Assyrian stele shows Esarhaddon holding a rope attached to an iron hook fastened into Taharka's jaw. The prophet Ezekiel referred to this practice.*

◀ *A side view of the Nineveh gateway.*

NERGAL GATE
MUSEUM

THE CAPTIVITY

Succession ▲   ▲ Daniel's Dreams

Chapter 17

JUDAH INTO EXILE

Hezekiah's son Manasseh was the worst king Judah ever had. He re-introduced Baal worship and set up an image of the fertility goddess in the temple, but he was converted and we can expect to see him in heaven. In 605 BC Nebuchadnezzar captured Jerusalem and sent Daniel and his companions into exile. Jerusalem was finally destroyed in 586 BC and most of the population sent into exile. There should be archaeological evidence for this depopulation but it is lacking at the end of the Iron Age where archaeologists are looking for it. There is plenty evidence for depopulation in the Late Bronze Period where the revised chronology would place it. Nebuchadnezzar aspired to make Babylon an eternal city but God gave him a symbolic dream, which Daniel interpreted to mean that three more kingdoms would follow Babylon. Nebuchadnezzar wrote the fourth chapter of the book of Daniel in which he told of a dream he had predicting his insanity for seven years. It happened and as a result Nebuchadnezzar was converted.

HEZEKIAH WAS SUCCEEDED BY HIS EVIL SON MANASSEH, who reinstated the worship of Baal and even installed a statue of the fertility goddess Asherah in the temple of God. He launched a period of savage persecution against those who maintained their fidelity to the true God. Jewish tradition claims that he had Isaiah put in a hollow log and sawn in half, which was probably why Paul referred to martyrs who "were sawn in two" (Heb. 11:37).

Incredibly, we can expect to meet Manasseh in heaven, a testimony to the unfathomable mercy of God to unworthy sinners. In the providence of God, Manasseh was captured by the Assyrian army, "who took Manasseh with hooks, bound him with bronze fetters, and carried him off to Babylon" (2 Chron. 33:11).

With a cruel iron hook in his jaw, Manasseh came to his senses. He "prayed to Him; and He received his entreaty, heard his supplication, and brought him back to Jerusalem into his kingdom. Then Manasseh knew that the Lord was God" (2 Chron. 33:13). He demonstrated his faith by ridding the land of all the foreign gods and restoring worship in the temple of Jerusalem.

Manasseh was succeeded by Amon and Josiah. The latter was another good king who instituted a great reformation in Judah, but he came to a strange end. Pharaoh Necho II of Egypt was apprehensive about the rising power of Babylon and marched his army to Carchemish on the Euphrates River to join with the remnants of the Assyrian army, who were fighting a rearguard battle against the Babylonians.

On the way to Carchemish, Necho was obliged to pass through land that belonged to Judah. Josiah marched against Necho, who sent him the message, "What have I to do with you, king of Judah? I have not come against you this day, but against the house with which I have war; for God commanded me to make haste. Refrain from meddling with God, who is with me, lest He destroy you" (2 Chron. 35:21).

Did God really speak to this heathen king rather than to his faithful servant Josiah? It would seem so, as Josiah persisted in his attack on the Egyptian army and was killed in the ensuing battle. It is not always easy to understand God's way. There are always factors we are not aware of.

DEFEAT AND DESTRUCTION

From here on Judah went downhill. Josiah was followed by Jehoahaz and Jehoiakim, in whose reign the Babylonians captured Jerusalem. In 625 B.C. Nabopolassar assumed the throne of Babylon and, in 612 B.C., in alliance with Cyaxeres the Mede, conquered Nineveh and burned it to the ground.

Nabopolassar deputed his army to his son Nebuchadnezzar, who besieged Jerusalem, but during the siege news reached him of his father's death in Babylon. Nebuchadnezzar hastened home to claim the throne, but Jerusalem was conquered in 605 B.C.

The prophet Jeremiah had pleaded with Jehoiakim to surrender to the Babylonians, warning that failure to do so would result in the destruction of the city. "He who remains in this city shall die by the sword, by famine, and by pestilence; but he who goes out and defects to the Chaldeans who besiege you, he shall live" (Jer. 21:9).

The Babylon gate rebuilt. ▼

▲ *Babylonian ruins adjacent to the city of Al Hilla.*

▲ *Ruins of the Ishtar gate, the eighth gate within the ancient city of Babylon.*

Jehoiakim stubbornly refused his pleas and Jeremiah predicted, "Thus says the Lord concerning Jehoiakim. . . . 'He shall be buried with the burial of a donkey, dragged and cast out beyond the gates of Jerusalem' " (Jer. 22:18–19). It turned out to be well beyond the gates of Jerusalem. "Nebuchadnezzar king of Babylon came up against him, and bound him in bronze fetters to carry him off to Babylon" (2 Chron. 36:6).

Jehoiakim's son Jehoiachin was only 18 years of age when he succeeded his father, but he was old enough to do "evil in the sight of the Lord, according to all that his father had done" (2 Kings 24:9). By the end of a three-month reign, Nebuchadnezzar had had enough of him. His army once more besieged Jerusalem, and Jehoiachin realized the game was up.

"Jehoiachin king of Judah, his mother, his servants, his princes, and his officers went out to the king of Babylon; and the king of Babylon, in the eighth year of his reign, took him prisoner" (2 Kings 24:12). The prophet Ezekiel was also among the captives taken to Babylon at this time. The Babylonians also took all the valuable treasures out of the temple and carried them off to Babylon, where they were later displayed in Belshazzar's drunken feast. The year was 597 B.C.

MERCY RECEIVED

In Babylon, Jehoiachin was imprisoned for 37 years, but when Nebuchadnezzar died he was replaced by his son Evil-Merodach, known in Babylon as Amel-Marduk, who for some unknown reason took a liking to Jehoiachin. He released him from prison and "spoke kindly to him, and gave him a more prominent seat than those of the kings who were with him in Babylon. So Jehoiachin changed from his prison garments, and he ate bread regularly before the king all the days of his life. And as for his provisions, there was a regular ration given him by the king, a portion for each day, all the days of his life" (2 Kings 25:28–30).

Strange that inspiration should bother to record such trivial details as the rations that were issued to the king, but archaeology demonstrated the value of this record.

When Professor Koldewey was excavating the debris near the Ishtar Gate of Babylon, he came across some cuneiform tablets that he sent back to Berlin. They lay on the shelves of the museum for 30 years until in 1933 George Weidner undertook the job of translating them. It was a boring task: receipts, commodities on hand, oil distributed, and rations given to prisoners.

Suddenly Weidner was electrified by what he read. "½ (PI) for Ya'kinu, king of the land of Ya(hu-du), 2½ sila for the fi(ve) sons of the king of the land of Yahuda, 4 sila for eight men Judeans."[1] (PI = 6 gallons, sila = 1½ pints.) The biblical details were not so insignificant after all.

> Then Nabuzaradan the captain of the guard carried away captive the rest of the people who remained in the city and the defectors who had deserted to the king of Babylon, with the rest of the multitude. But the captain of the guard left some of the poor of the land as vinedressers and farmers (2 Kings 25:11–12).

What with those who had been sent into exile by the Assyrians and those who had been deported to Babylon, the land must have been almost emptied of its inhabitants, and there ought to be some archaeological evidence for it. There is, but not at the time most archaeologists are looking for it.

CHRONOLOGY

By the traditional chronology, the Israelites came into Palestine at the beginning of the Early Iron Age about 1200 B.C., which is not the biblical date anyway. According to the Bible, Joshua conquered Jericho about 1405 B.C., not

---

1.   D. Winton Thomas, *Documents from Old Testament Times* (New York: Harper, 1961), p. 86.

▲ *Reconstructed entrance to Nebuchadnezzar's palace.*

1200. The fall of Jerusalem would have been at the end of the Iron Age II, 539 B.C., but there was no sign of depopulation at that time.

In my view, the Middle Bronze Age should be recognized as the period of Israelite occupation, and the following Late Bronze Age the period of exile. There is plenty evidence for this.

Israel Finkelstein wrote a book called *The Archaeology of the Israelite Settlement,* in which he said:

> The entire country flourished in MB IIB. . . . The fortified centers of the hill country, as well as many of the cities of the lowlands, were destroyed at the end of the Middle Bronze II. . . . In contrast to the extraordinary prosperity of MB II, the Late Bronze period was characterized by a severe crisis in settlement. . . . Moreover, those sites where occupation did continue frequently shrank in size.
>
> The Iron I period again witnessed a dramatic swing in the population of the hill country, this time in the opposite direction. . . . MB II, Late Bronze and Iron I periods . . . leave two critical questions for which satisfactory answers must be found. Why and to where did over half of the MB II population, i.e., virtually all the inhabitants of the hill country, vanish? From where did the people who settled the hundreds of sites in Iron I materialize?[2]

Could anything be plainer?

MBII: prosperity at the time of David, Solomon, Israel, and Judah

LB: depopulation resulting from the exile

2.   Israel Finkelstein, *The Archaeology of the Israelite Settlement* (Jerusalem: Israel Exploration Society, 1988), p. 339–341.

Iron Age I: repopulation after the exile

This would also explain why Israeli archaeologists can find so little evidence for the Persian Period. They are looking for it at the end of Iron Age II. It is not there. They should be looking at the beginning of Iron Age I when all these people were suddenly turning up in Israel.

Some have suggested that at the end of MBII the population suddenly decided it was time to move out of the cities and enjoy some country living. But at the end of Late Bronze they decided it was not such a good idea after all, and all moved back into the cities. An unlikely scenario and, in any case, there would have been evidence for all these people in the country. There is none.

THE GOLDEN CITY

Nebuchadnezzar was a remarkable king. It was his ambition to build a city that would never be conquered and start a dynasty that would never end. In this he was to be sadly disappointed. Though Babylon is termed in the Bible as "the golden city" (Isa. 14:4), the Babylonian Empire lasted a shorter period of time than any of the other great empires of the Middle East, only 66 years.

One night Nebuchadnezzar fell asleep pondering the future and had an impressive dream. When he awakened in the morning he knew he had seen this dream but could not remember what it was he had dreamed. So he called in his wise men in whom he had implicit confidence, and demanded that they tell him what he had dreamed and explain its meaning to him. "Then the Chaldeans spoke to the king in Aramaic, 'O king, live forever! Tell your servants the dream and we will give the interpretation' " (Dan. 2:4). The Babylonians attached a lot of importance to dreams and the wise men could always cook up some

The remains of what was Nebuchadnezzar's palace. ▶

interpretation, but of course they could not tell the king what he had dreamed.

The king was furious. He had such confidence in their ability that he thought they knew what he had dreamed but were just playing for time, so he decreed that they all be put to death. This, however, included Daniel and his companions. When Daniel learned of this death decree he asked to see the king and "asked the king to give him time, that he might tell the king the interpretation" (Dan. 2:16).

That night God gave Daniel the same dream and in the morning he approached the king and said, "There is a God in heaven who reveals secrets, and he has made known to King Nebuchadnezzar what will be in the latter days" (Dan. 2:28). That was just what the king wanted to know, though he was doomed to disappointment.

DREAM REVEALED

Daniel went on to say, "You, O king, were watching; and behold, a great image. . . . This image's head was of fine gold, its chest and arms of silver, its belly and thighs of bronze, its legs of iron, its feet partly of iron and partly of clay. You watched while a stone was cut out without hands, which struck the image on its feet of iron and clay, and broke them in pieces" (Dan. 2:31–34).

Then Daniel told the king the meaning of his dream. "You are this head of gold" (verse 38). That would have been pleasing to Nebuchadnezzar, but then came the bad news. "After you shall arise another kingdom inferior to yours; then another, a third kingdom of bronze" (verse 39).

History testifies to the accuracy of the prophecy. In 539 B.C. the Medo-Persians conquered Babylon, and in 331 B.C. Alexander the Great routed Darius III and ushered in the Greek period.

Daniel continued, "The fourth kingdom shall be strong as iron" (verse 40). In 168 B.C. at the battle of Pydna, the Romans defeated the Greeks and ushered in the iron monarchy of Rome.

Rome held sway until A.D. 476 when it succumbed to the Barbarian invasions, symbolized by the feet of iron and of clay. "The kingdom shall be divided" (verse 41). There was to be no fifth kingdom.

The historian Edward Gibbon wrote, "The arms of the republic, sometimes vanquished in battle, always victorious in war, advanced with rapid steps to the Euphrates, the Danube, the Rhine, and the ocean, and the images of gold, silver or brass, that might serve to represent the nations and their kings, were successively broken by the iron monarchy of Rome."[3]

Nebuchadnezzar was impressed, but after a while his ambitions to establish an eternal kingdom returned and he set up an image all of gold for people to worship. There were to be no kingdoms of silver, bronze, or iron, but God did not give up on Nebuchadnezzar. In fact, Nebuchadnezzar wrote a chapter of the Bible in which he tells of his conversion, and it seems likely that we can expect to meet Nebuchadnezzar in heaven.

In chapter 4, Daniel tells of how the king became an imbecile for seven years, but Nebuchadnezzar got the message. At the end of this time he wrote, "Now I, Nebuchadnezzar, praise and extol and honor the King of heaven, all of whose works are truth, and His ways justice. And those who walk in pride He is able to put down" (Dan. 4:37).

Some may wonder how the Babylonians could maintain their loyalty to a king who was an imbecile for seven years, but many Eastern people take a different view of abnormalities and mental illness. The Egyptians greatly admired dwarfs and some were promoted to high positions in state. I once saw a man in India leading around a cow that had five legs, one dangling uselessly from its belly, and he was making a good living out of this abnormality. Cows are regarded as sacred by most Hindus.

Among the Tibetans I once saw a mentally deranged man. His fellow Tibetans regarded him with awe. The Babylonians apparently shared this attitude and patiently waited until their monarch returned to normal.

3.   Edward Gibbon, *The Decline and Fall of the Roman Empire* (UK: Sadler & Brown, 1967).

THE MEDO-PERSIAN EMPIRE

Belshazzar Rules

Rebuilding Jerusalem

Chapter 18

RETURN FROM EXILE

Nabonidus was the last king of Babylon but he had crowned his son Belshazzar as his co-regent king while he was on military activities outside Babylon. Cyrus the Persian diverted the waters of the Euphrates that ran through Babylon and marched his troops up the near dry river bed. They occupied Babylon and killed Belshazzar. Darius the Mede subsequently presided over Babylon. Cyrus' conquest of Babylon had been predicted by the prophet Isaiah. Cyrus issued a decree allowing the Jews to return to Jerusalem and rebuild the temple. The Cyrus cylinder supports this record. Cyrus was succeeded by Cambyses, Smerdis, and Darius I who became the greatest of the Persian kings. He left a record of his accession on the face of the Zagros Mountain at Bisitun. The inscription was in three languages, which enabled scholars to decipher the cuneiform script. The enemies of the Jews did much to prevent the rebuilding of the walls of Jerusalem but with the help of the prophets the work was finally completed.

DANIEL

NEBUCHADNEZZAR WAS SUCCEEDED BY HIS SON Amel Marduk, who had reigned for only two years, 562–560 B.C., when he was assassinated. His brother Nergal-shar-usur took his place but ruled for only four years, 560–556 B.C. Then came his son Labashi-Marduk, who was also assassinated after only two months on the throne.

The last king of Babylon was Nabonidus. This rather embarrassed some Bible believers because of the story of Belshazzar and the writing on the wall, which gave the impression that Belshazzar was the last king of Babylon. They should have noted that Belshazzar offered to promote anyone who could interpret the writing on the wall to be "the third ruler in the kingdom" (Dan. 5:7). Nabonidus was the first, Belshazzar was the second, and whoever could explain the writing could only be the third.

Belshazzar was the son of Nabonidus, who was an unusual character. His mother was a priestess of the moon god Sin, and Nabonidus had tried to introduce this worship into Babylon. But the Babylonians did not take kindly to this innovation and Nabonidus was not very popular. He found it more congenial to conduct military operations outside Babylon. He actually spent about ten years in Arabia. He was on the battlefield around Babylon when the city fell to Cyrus.

The prophet Isaiah had predicted this last night of Babylonian supremacy 150 years before it all happened. He wrote, "Thus says the Lord to his anointed [literally his Messiah], to Cyrus . . . to open before him the double doors, so that the gates will not be shut" (Isa. 45:1).

BABYLON FALLS

Cyrus was a great military leader who had already occupied Anatolia and Mesopotamia. In 539 B.C. he turned his attention to Babylon. He well knew the invincibility of Babylon's massive double walls, so he diverted the waters of the River Euphrates, which ran through the center of Babylon, then marched his troops along the near-empty river bed on the occasion of Babylon's pagan festival.

Even then it could have been a futile exercise. The walls flanking the river had strong gates that were normally closed to prevent access to the city, but during this drunken festival the guards had neglected to close them, and Cyrus's soldiers were able to enter the city unopposed. "That very night Belshazzar, king of the Chaldeans, was slain. And Darius the Mede received the kingdom" (Dan. 5:30–31).

Darius did not "take" the kingdom. He only "received" it. This was the Medo-Persian Empire. Cyrus the Persian was the military commander who took the kingdom and deputed Darius the Mede to care for Babylon.

No doubt Daniel acquainted Cyrus with the prophecy that foretold his conquest of Babylon because he issued a decree allowing the exiles to return to their home countries. "He made a proclamation throughout all his kingdom, and also put it in writing saying, 'Thus says Cyrus king of Persia: All the kingdoms of the earth the Lord [Yehovah]

The tomb of Cyrus the Great of Persia. ▼

▲ *Looking out over the Zagros Mountain at Bisitun, Iraq.*

▲ *The record of accession on the face of the Zagros Mountain at Bisitun.*

God of heaven has given me. And he has commanded me to build Him a house at Jerusalem" (Ezra 1:1–2).

The record of the decree allowing exiles to return to their home countries was found in a cylinder that was discovered in the gateway of Babylon. It is partially damaged but much is legible. It says, "I am Cyrus, king of the world, great king, legitimate king, king of Babylon, king of Sumer and Akkad, king of the four rims (of the earth). . . . All the kings of the entire world from the Upper to the Lower Sea, those who are seated in throne rooms, (those who) live in other (types of buildings as well as) all the kings of the West land living in tents, brought their heavy tributes and kissed my feet in Babylon. (As to the region) from . . . as far as Ashur and Susa, Agade, Eshnunna, the towns Zamban, Me-Turnu, Der as well as the region of the Gutians, I returned to (these) sacred cities on the other side of the Tigris, the sanctuaries which have been ruins for a long time, the images which (used) to live therein and established for them permanent sanctuaries. I (also) gathered all their (former) inhabitants and returned (to them) their habitations."[1]

So the return from exile began, but the number who chose to return was pitifully small. Most of the families had settled down in their new environment and were reluctant to leave. But the noble group under Zerubbabel reached Jerusalem and laid the foundation for the temple, and reinstated the religious rites and annual festivals. But opposition soon arose. Their enemies "hired counselors against them to frustrate their purpose all the days of Cyrus king of Persia, even until the reign of Darius king of Persia" (Ezra 4:5).

DARIUS TAKES THE THRONE

Cyrus was succeeded by his son Cambyses, who invaded Egypt and remained there for three years. There is some uncertainty about the details of the reign of Cambyses, but it seems that to make sure his popular brother Bardiya, also known as Smerdis, did not seize the throne in his absence, he had him put to death. When Cambyses did decide to return to Persia he died on the way. An impostor by the name of Gaumata announced that he was the son of Cyrus who was supposed to have been killed, and with the help of his subordinates he mounted the throne. He has become known as the False Smerdis.

He lasted only six months, when his officers became dissatisfied with his rule. One of them by the name of Darius managed to gain access to his harem and assassinated him. Darius then had to establish his authority over the governors of the provinces. He left a record of his accession to the throne in three languages on the face of the Zagros mountain at a place called Bisitun. It has become known as the Behistun Rock, and this inscription played an important role in the deciphering of the cuneiform script.

In 1835 Sir Henry Rawlinson, who was at the time an officer of the British East India Company, decided to make a squeeze of the inscription. When the writers of the inscription worked on it they started at the top and worked down, made a ledge at the bottom, then cut away the rock face below it. Rawlinson was not able to climb up to the ledge. He had to have some assistants lower him on ropes from above. Back home, Rawlinson worked on the Persian in which he was very fluent, and by comparison he was able to decipher the Elamite and Akkadian.

In 1958 I visited this rock for the first time, not dreaming I would be able to reach the ledge, but over to the left I noticed a vertical aperture in the rock. I managed to squeeze myself up this aperture until I came to a crack in the rock that slanted upward to the right.

Fortunately the rock face was not exactly vertical, and by leaning against it I was able to ease along until I could get my fingers over the ledge. The rest was easy. I could get some good pictures of this remarkable inscription that has

1.   Geoffrey W. Bromiley, *International Standard Bible Encyclopedia, Vol. 1* (Grand Rapids, MI: W.B. Eerdmans, 1979, 1988), p. 846–847.

survived weathering for 2,500 years. Originally the symbols cut into the rock were filled with lead. Thieves have long since stolen the lead, but the letters are still remarkably clear.

CONSTRUCTION HALTED

During the reign of the False Smerdis, called Artaxerxes in Ezra 4, Israel's enemies wrote a letter pointing out that Jerusalem had been a rebellious city in the past, and advising the king to halt the work of rebuilding. The Persian ruler looked into the matter and found the accusation to be justified, so he ordered the rebuilding to cease. The Jews were obliged to stop their work.

Actually, under the decree of Cyrus they were quite entitled to rebuild, so the prophets Haggai and Zechariah urged them to resume their work.

> In the second year of King Darius . . . the word of the Lord came by Haggai the prophet, saying, "Is it time for you yourselves to dwell in your paneled houses, and this temple to lie in ruins?" Now

◀ *Bas-relief of Mede and Persian nobility.*

▲ *The ancient city of Persepolis, which was known as the city of Persians.* ▼

therefore, thus says the Lord of hosts: "Consider your ways!" (Hag. 1:1–5).

They got the message and resumed their building. Authorities demanded an explanation, so the builders told them that it was Cyrus who had issued the first decree allowing them to rebuild. That settled the matter. By this time Cyrus had just about become deified in Persia, and when a search was made in Babylon and Achmetha (Hamadan), and the decree of Cyrus was found, permission to continue building was soon given by Darius.

The reign of Darius was a glorious epoch in the history of Persia. He built the magnificent city of Persepolis, which is today regarded as the pearl of Middle East ruins. The opulence of his court has hardly been excelled since.

JERUSALEM'S TRIUMPH

Xerxes Rules ▲   ▲ The Temple Completed

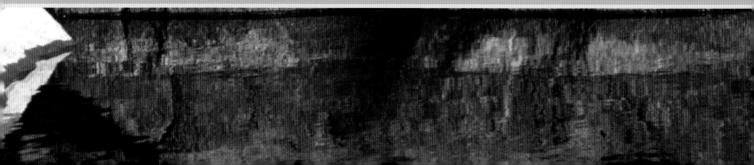

Chapter 19

ESTHER TO MALACHI

Xerxes followed his father Darius on the throne of Persia. He proposed a massive invasion of Greece, but his Greek campaign was a disaster. On his return he sought a replacement for Vashti and the Jewish girl Esther was chosen. Haman was the king's deputy and because Mordecai the Jew would not bow down before him he asked the king to sign a decree to annihilate all the Jews in the kingdom. Esther organized a banquet to reveal to the king that she and her people were to be annihilated. When the king heard this he was furious and had Haman hanged. This deliverance is still celebrated by Jewish people in the annual festival of Purim. With the help of Ezra and Nehemiah the temple and city walls were finally completed. This temple, though not as magnificent as the temple built by Solomon, was actually greater because Jesus Christ, the Son of God, graced the building with His presence.

ESTHER

DARIUS WAS SUCCEEDED BY HIS SON XERXES, KNOWN in the Bible as Ahasuerus, who planned a massive invasion of Greece. Probably to get his nation on his side he "made a feast for all his officials and servants" (Esther 1:3). It lasted 180 days, and to top it off he threw a seven-day feast for all the people in Shushan where his court was at the time. It was a grand display of the empire's fabulous wealth. "There were white and blue curtains fastened with cords of fine linen and purple on silver rods and marble pillars; and the couches were of gold and silver on a mosaic pavement of alabaster, turquoise, and white and black marble. And they served drinks in golden vessels, each vessel being different from the other" (Esther 1:6–7).

Archaeology has provided interesting evidence of this. Several of these drinking vessels have been found. Called rhytons, they are of exquisite workmanship and are all completely different from each other.

It was during this drinking bout that Xerxes decided to display his queen's beauty to his courtiers and sent a message for her to come to his drinking party. The virtuous queen Vashti refused to come to be put on display before these vulgar males. The king was incensed that his queen did not obey his command so he deposed her. He then embarked on his massive Greek campaign that ended in disaster for the Persian army. On his return, Xerxes sought for a new queen and the Jewish girl Esther was chosen, though the king was not aware of her ethnic origin.

> After these things King Ahasuerus promoted Haman . . . and set his seat above all the princes who were with him. And all the king's servants who were within the king's gate bowed and paid homage to Haman, for so the king had commanded concerning him (Esther 3:1–2).

HAMAN'S PLOT AGAINST THE JEWS

Esther's parents had died and she had been brought up by her cousin Mordecai, a strict Jew who refused to prostrate himself before a human being. When this was reported to Haman he was "filled with wrath" (Esther 3:5), and he determined to wipe out all the Jews in the realm. Xerxes acceded to Haman's petition and a decree was issued requiring all the Jews to be annihilated on the day specified.

Mordecai brought this to Esther's notice and pointed out that as a Jew, she also would be killed. He advised her to intercede with the king to have the decree revoked. It was not customary for the queen to approach the king unless she had been summoned, but Esther agreed, saying, "If I perish, I perish!" (Esther 4:16).

"So it was, when the king saw Queen Esther standing in the court, that she found favor in his sight, and the king held out to Esther the golden scepter that was in his hand" (Esther 5:2). Reliefs in Persepolis depict the Persian king with a scepter in his hand. Such a scene is not portrayed in other Eastern countries.

Esther requested the king to come with Haman to a banquet she had prepared. The king agreed and he and Haman went to the feast. Of course the king knew there was something behind this request, but he was in a good mood and asked Esther what

An ancient metallic case for storing the scroll of Esther. ▼

▲ Elaphantine Island in Eygpt where Jews built a second temple.

▲ "Ahasuerus and Haman at Esther's Feast," by Rembrandt (1660).

she wanted, with the customary promise to give her anything she wanted up to half his kingdom. The queen only requested that he and Haman should come to another feast she was preparing for the next day. The king readily agreed.

Haman felt duly flattered that he should be invited to a feast with the king in his harem, but passing through the city gate on his way home from the feast, "when Haman saw Mordecai in the king's gate, and that he did not stand or tremble before him, he was filled with indignation against Mordecai" (Esther 5:9).

When he returned to his home he proudly told his family of the honor that he had received but added, "Yet all this avails me nothing, so long as I see Mordecai the Jew sitting at the king's gate" (Esther 5:13). His family and friends suggested that he erect a gallows and have Mordecai hanged on it. It seemed like a good idea and Haman ordered the gallows to be erected.

HAMAN'S PLOT BACKFIRES

That night the king could not sleep, so he ordered someone to read to him from the court chronicles. That should have been boring enough to put anyone to sleep, but during the reading the king noticed the record that two men had been plotting against his life. Mordecai had heard of the plot and reported it to the authorities, and the king's life was saved.

Regicide (the killing of a king) was common in Persia. Many of the Persian kings were assassinated, so the king felt grateful that his life had been spared. He asked what reward had been given to Mordecai and found that he had received no reward for his act. The next morning Haman came early to ask the king's permission to hang Mordecai, but before he could speak the king asked him, "What shall be done for the man whom the king delights to honor?" (Esther 6:6).

Haman was naïve enough to imagine that the king was about to honor him, and he suggested that such a one should be arrayed in royal robes and paraded through the city on the king's horse. The king readily agreed and told Haman to get Mordecai and bestow this honor upon him. The humiliated Haman was obliged to do as the king commanded.

That day the king and Haman went to Esther's second banquet, and at its conclusion the king again asked Esther what was her request. Esther replied, "If it pleases the king, let my life be given me at my petition, and my people at my request. For we have been sold, my people and I, to be destroyed" (Esther 7:3–4).

The king was shocked to think that anyone would dare to lay hands on his beautiful queen, and asked, "Who is he, and where is he, who would dare presume in his heart to do such a thing?" Pointing her slender finger at Haman, Esther replied, "This wicked Haman!" (Esther 7:5–6).

The king was so horrified that he rose and went out to the palace garden to consider his next move. Haman was terrified at the disclosure and fell on Esther's couch pleading for mercy. When the king returned and saw Haman on the queen's couch he asked, "Will he also assault the queen while I am in the house?" (Esther 7:8). An official standing nearby thought it an appropriate moment to mention to the king that Haman had erected an 82-foot (25 meter) high gallows on which to hang Mordecai. "Hang him on it!" the king roared.

But there was still the decree to kill all the Jews, and the laws of the Medes and Persians could not be changed. The king's solution was to issue a second decree authorizing the Jews to defend themselves, and even to kill any who dared to attack them. Mordecai was promoted to replace Haman, but the whole incident was undoubtedly allowed by God as a warning to the Jews to return to their homeland or face the perils of staying in foreign countries.

PURIM CELEBRATED TODAY

This incident has now become a regular annual celebration in the Jewish calendar. It is called Purim and is celebrated on the 14th and 15th days of the Jewish month of Adar,

around March each year. It is celebrated by feasting and merriment, wearing masks and costumes, almsgiving, sending food to neighbors and friends, and chanting the text of Esther.

The Book of Esther is unique in the Bible. It is the only biblical book that does not mention the word *God*, which may suggest it was copied from Persian archives, possibly by Mordecai himself. Esther 10:2 says that the record of Ahasuerus and Mordecai were "written in the book of the chronicles of the kings of Media and Persia." The longest verse in the Bible, 83 English words, is found in Esther 8:9.

In 465 B.C., Xerxes was assassinated, probably by orders of his son Artaxerxes. He was buried in his tomb alongside other Persian kings at a site near Persepolis. Recently his tomb was in the news because of a proposed railway line to be built near it. Public outcry demanded the line be built elsewhere. Authorities agreed to place it about 500 feet (150 meters) farther away, but there is still fear that vibrations will cause the collapse of the spur into which his tomb was dug.

EZRA AND NEHEMIAH

In 457 B.C., Ezra, a learned and pious scribe living in Babylon, gathered a company of exiles to make the journey to Jerusalem. He was armed with a decree from Artaxerxes that not only permitted the completion of the temple but provided financial assistance for them to do so. It also authorized the appointments of magistrates and judges, giving virtual legislative independence to Israel.

When the heads were counted, Ezra was disappointed to find that there were no Levites among them, so he made a special appeal to the Levites in exile. When they responded, the company set out on their tedious journey. Ezra showed his faith in divine protection by refusing a military guard to escort them on the way. He said, "The hand of our God is upon all those for good who seek him" (Ezra 8:22).

Nehemiah held the trusted position of cupbearer to King Artaxerxes in Shushan. Some men who had been in Jerusalem returned to Persia, and Nehemiah questioned them concerning the rebuilding of the city. He was distressed to learn that the work had ground to a halt and some of the walls that had been rebuilt had been broken down.

◀ *Rock carved tomb of the Persian king Darius the Great.*

Tomb of the Persian King ▶
(close-up)

The tomb of Esther and Mordechai is located in Hamadan, Iran. ▼

The king noticed his apparent anxiety and asked him the reason, adding, "This is nothing but sorrow of heart" (Neh. 2:2). This made Nehemiah "terribly afraid." The king was inferring that there was some plot to poison the king that made Nehemiah look anxious. Nehemiah hastily acquainted the king with the reason for his sorrow and requested permission of the king to go to Jerusalem to supervise the rebuilding of the walls. The king acceded to his request and Nehemiah set out on his journey.

Arriving in Jerusalem, Nehemiah at first did not disclose his mission but secretly at night straddled a donkey and did the rounds of the walls. He was distressed at what he saw and proceeded to encourage the residents to resume their building. "But when Sanballat the Horonite, Tobiah the Ammonite official, and Geshem the Arab heard of it, they laughed at us and despised us" (Neh. 2:19). They took active measures to hinder the rebuilding. These officials are known to archaeologists.

SANBALLAT, TOBIAH, AND GESHEM IDENTIFIED

In the middle of the River Nile at Aswan is an island about a mile (1.5 km) in length, called Elephantine Island. The island probably derived its name from the appearance of some clumps of rocks that look like herds of elephants. On this island archaeologists found the remains of a Jewish synagogue in which were discovered some papyrus documents written in several languages including Aramaic.

It is likely that this Jewish colony originated with a group of Jews who fled from Jerusalem at the time of its destruction by Babylon in 576 B.C. Jeremiah warned them not to go to Egypt, but they went anyway. Moses had said there was to be only one temple for Israel to worship in, but these people considered it impossible to go that far so they requested permission from the authorities in Jerusalem to build a temple at Elephantine.

Sanballat was an enemy to be reckoned with. He was the governor of Samaria, appointed by the Persian government, no doubt with an army at his disposal.

One letter had been written about 525 B.C. to Bagoas, the governor of Judea at the time. It concluded by saying, "We sent in our name all these words in one letter to Delaiah and Shelamiah sons of Sanballat governor of Samaria."[1]

---

1. James W. Watts, editor, *Persia and Torah: The Theory of Imperial Authorization of the Pentateuch* (Atlanta, GA: Society of Biblical Literature, 2001), p. 103.

▲ *The prophets revenge tomb of Zechariah in the Kidron Valley in Jerusalem.*

The reference to Sanballat was probably an inference that if permission was not forthcoming from authorities in Jerusalem they would appeal to the Samaritans for support.

Tobiah was actually a Hebrew name meaning "Yehovah is good," and he had managed to secure a room for his use in the new temple (Neh. 13:5). Halfway between Jericho and Amman are some ruins called Iraq el Emir, and inscribed on the wall of a cave included in this estate is the name Tobiah. Apparently Tobiah was the head of a wealthy family on the east side of the Jordan River.

In the Brooklyn Museum in America is a silver vessel on which there is an Aramaic inscription that mentions Qaimu, son of Geshem king of Kedar, an Arab tribe often mentioned in the Bible (Isa. 21:16 and other texts). As the Aramaic inscription can be dated to the late fifth century B.C., about the time Nehemiah was in Jerusalem, it can be safely concluded that the Geshem mentioned by Nehemiah was an important tribal king who would have posed a real threat to the builders in Jerusalem.

TRIUMPH AT LAST

But despite all the opposition, the temple and walls were finally completed. The new temple was but a shadow of the magnificent temple built by Solomon, and some who were alive to see Solomon's temple in its glory wept when they saw this later model. But Haggai had predicted, "I will shake all nations, and the desire of all nations shall come: and I will fill this house with glory, saith the Lord of hosts" (Hag. 2:7; KJV).

The presence of Israel's promised Messiah in this second temple would more than compensate for the inferior building. He would bring salvation and eternal life, not just to the children of Abraham but to a lost world.

In the days of Zerubbabel, Zechariah saw in prophetic vision the triumphal entry into Jerusalem and the enthusiastic crowd shouting, "Rejoice greatly, O daughter of Zion! Shout, O daughter of Jerusalem! Behold, your King is coming to you; He is just and having salvation, lowly and riding on a donkey" (Zech. 9:9).

Then he was horrified to behold the base betrayal of the Messiah as Judas bargained with the Pharisees over the amount they would pay him to betray his master. "Then I said to them, 'If it is agreeable to you, give me my wages; and if not, refrain.' So they weighed out for my wages thirty pieces of silver" (Zech. 11:12).

In that vast host of the redeemed who are resurrected to eternal life will be some who have never heard about the crucifixion of Christ, but they have lived up to the light they had in helping the poor and showing kindness to the needy, and Jesus accepts them as His children. In awe they behold the majestic form of the Son of God, but they notice His wounded hands. "And one will say to him, 'What are these wounds between your arms?' Then he will answer, 'Those with which I was wounded in the house of my friends' " (Zech. 13:6).

The prophet Malachi wrote the last chapter in the Old Testament, and he also rejoiced to foresee the coming of the Messiah. Through him the divine promise was given: "To you who fear My name the Sun of Righteousness shall arise with healing in his wings" (Mal. 4:2).

The promise was fulfilled. "God anointed Jesus of Nazareth with the Holy Spirit and with power, who went about doing good and healing all who were oppressed by the devil, for God was with Him" (Acts 10:38).

BIBLICAL EVENTS & REFERENCE		KING
United Monarchy of Israel		
Samuel tells Saul his kingdom shall end	I Samuel 13:13–14	Saul
God has Samuel to annoint David as king	I Samuel 16:12-13	David
David makes Solomon king	I Kings 1:43	Solomon
Kingdom of Judah		
David places Rehoboam in Bethel	I Kings 12:29a	Rehoboam
Abijah takes over for Rehoboam	2 Chronicles 12:16	Abijah
Asa takes over for Abijah	I Kings 15:8	Asa
Jehoshaphat takes over for Asa	I Kings 22:41	Jehoshaphat
Jehoram takes over for Jehoshaphat	2 Chronicles 21:1	Jehoram
Ahaziah takes over for Jehoram	2 Chronicles 22:1	Ahaziah
Ahaziah's mother Athaliah tries to end seed	2 Kings 11:1	Athaliah
Ahaziah's sister hides his son, Jehoash	2 Kings 11:2	Jehoash
Amaziah reigns after Jehoash's murder	2 Kings 12:21	Amaziah
16-year-old Uzziah named king by people	2 Kings 14:21	Uzziah
Jotham rules after father's death	2 Kings 15:7	Jotham
20-year-old Ahaz reigned for 16 years	2 Kings 16:2	Ahaz
Hezekiah takes over for Ahaz	2 Kings 16:20	Hezekiah
12-year-old Manasseh reigns 55 years	2 Kings 21:1	Manasseh
Amon takes over for Manasseh	2 Kings 21:18	Amon
8-year-old Josiah reigned 31 years	2 Kings 22:1	Josiah
Jehoahaz anointed king in his father's stead	2 Kings 23:30	Jehoahaz
Jehoiakim reigns for eleven years	2 Kings 23:36	Jehoiakim
18-year-old Jehoiachin reigns	2 Kings 21:1	Jehoiachin
City beseiged during Zedekiah's reign	2 Kings 25:2	Zedekiah
Kingdom of Israel		
David places Jeroboam in Dan	I Kings 12:29b	Jeroboam
Nadab takes over for Jeroboam	I Kings 14:20	Nadab
Baasha slayed Asa and reigned in his stead	I Kings 15:28	Baasha
Elah takes over for Baasha	I Kings 16:6	Elah
Zimri reigns 7 days in Tirzah	I Kings 16:15	Zimri
Israel divided over Tibni and Omri	I Kings 16:21	Tibni
Omri defeats Tibni and reigns alone	I Kings 16:22	Omri
Ahab takes over for Omri	I Kings 16:28	Ahab
Ahaziah replaces Ahab at the throne	I Kings 22:40	Ahaziah
Jehoram, son of Ahab, reigns	2 Kings 3:1	Jehoram
Jehu anointed king	I Kings 19:16	Jehu
Jehoahaz takes over for Jehu	I Kings 14:20	Jehoahaz
Jehoash reigns for 40 years	2 Kings 12:1	Jehoash
Jeroboam II takes over Jehoash's throne	2 Kings 13:13	Jeroboam II
Zechariah takes over for Jeroboam II	2 Kings 15:8	Zechariah
Shallum rises up against Zechariah	2 Kings 15:10	Shallum
Menahem slew Shallum	2 Kings 15:14	Menahem
Pekahiah takes over for Menahem	2 Kings 15:22-3	Pekahiah
Pekah begins his reign	2 Kings 15:27	Pekah
The Word of the Lord came unto Hosea	Hosea 1:1	Hosea

THE EVERLASTING REIGN

Fulfillment ▲   ▲ Ultimate Victory

Chapter 20

KING OF KINGS

From the first prophetic words in Genesis 3:15, spoken by God to the serpent concerning the One to come who would crush the serpent's head, the Old Testament is filled with insights into the coming Messiah; the King of kings. Jesus Himself explained these passages to some of His followers beginning with the writings of Moses (Luke 24:27). He is the king that God always intended to lead His people to peace, though His earthly life began in the most humble of circumstances.

WHEN KING ZEDEKIAH WAS DEPOSED BY THE Babylonians in 586 BC it seemed that Israel's monarchy had come to an end, but King David had been told by God, "Your throne shall be established forever," (2 Sam. 7:16), and Isaiah had written, "Unto us a Child is born, Unto us a Son is given; And the government will be upon His shoulder. And His name will be called Wonderful, Counselor, Mighty God, Everlasting Father, Prince of Peace" (Isa. 8:6).

More than five hundred years rolled by and there was no sign of its fulfillment, but "with the Lord one day is as a thousand years, and a thousand years as one day (2 Pet. 3:6). So "when the fullness of the time had come, God sent forth His Son, born of a woman" (Gal. 4:4). That woman was Mary. The angel of the Lord appeared to her and informed her that she was to bear a son and she was to call his name Jesus. "He will be great, and will be called the Son of the Highest; and the Lord God will give Him the throne of His father David. And He will reign over the house of Jacob forever, and of His kingdom there will be no end" (Luke 1:32,33).

To avoid embarrassment, Mary decided to leave Nazareth and stay with her relative Elizabeth who lived in Judea. This would have been a long and arduous journey on foot along the Plain of Jezreel to the Jordan Valley, which she would follow to Jericho, and then up the hills to Jerusalem. Where exactly Elizabeth lived in Judea is not known. Mary would not have been able to make this journey alone. She must have walked with others who were making a similar journey. Elizabeth gave birth to John (the Baptist), and Mary returned after that to Nazareth.

In the meantime, word had reached Joseph that the woman to whom he was betrothed was pregnant. By the law of Moses she should have been stoned to death (Deut. 22:13–21). But "Joseph her husband, being a just man, and not wanting to make her a public example, was minded to put her away secretly. But while he thought about these things, behold, an angel of the Lord appeared to him in a dream, saying, 'Joseph, son of David, do not be afraid to take to you Mary your wife, for that which is conceived in her is of the Holy Spirit'" (Matt. 1:19,20). Awesome, that God the Father should allow His Son to adopt humanity, and that His Son should be willing to step down from His majestic throne and become a mortal man, unrecognized and despised by most.

Joseph and Mary would have expected the baby to be born in Nazareth, but Bible prophecy had decreed otherwise. The prophet Micah, who came from Mareshah had written, "But you, Bethlehem Ephrathah, though you are little among the thousands of Judah, yet out of you shall come forth to Me the One to be Ruler in Israel" (Micah 5:2). Mareshah is only 20 kilometers from Bethlehem, and I and my group of volunteers have excavated there annually for the last ten years.

Hundreds of miles away in imperial Rome, the emperor Caesar Augustus issued a decree "that all the world should be registered" (Luke 2:1). Joseph's ancestors came from Bethlehem so he was obliged to travel there. Artists usually depict Mary riding on a donkey, but the humble carpenter was unlikely to have been able to afford such a luxury. It is more likely that the heavily pregnant Mary would have had to make the long journey on foot.

▼ *The Magi brought gifts of gold, frankincense, and myrrh.*

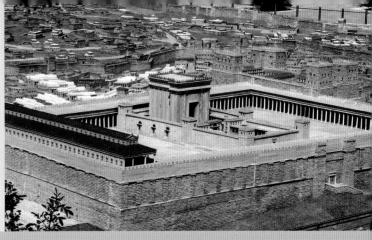

▲ Ruins of ancient basilica on Shepherds Fields in Beit Sahour, a Palestinian town east of Bethlehem, Palestine.

▲ A model of second temple that was built after return from Exile. It was embellished by Herod the Great and Jesus worshipped in this temple.

Arriving at Bethlehem they found that all accommodation was fully occupied. They were obliged to take shelter in the village caravanserai, a walled enclosure with facilities for animals for temporary visitors. It was here that the royal child was born and placed on the straw in a manger. The location is not known. The Church of the Nativity in Bethlehem incorporates a traditional site that has no historical value. Angels appeared to the shepherds on the fields around Bethlehem. They sang the beautiful song, "Glory to God in the highest, and on earth peace, goodwill toward men!" (Luke 2:14).

About forty days later, after Jesus' dedication at the temple, "wise men from the East came to Jerusalem saying, "Where is He who has been born King of the Jews? For we have seen His star in the East and have come to worship Him" (Matt. 2:1–2). They were Magi, philosophers from Persia to whom God had spoken.

When Herod heard of their errand he was disturbed. He was the king of the Jews and would not tolerate any contender. When the magi did not return he sent his soldiers to kill all the babies in Bethlehem. The people of Bethlehem had given scant regard to the report of the shepherds and God did not interpose to protect their babies.

Archeologists have detailed information about the life of King Herod but there is no record of this incident. It is however consistent with what we know of his suspicious character. He murdered many of his own relatives on suspicion they were aspiring to his throne. Herod died soon after this incident and was buried in the Herodion near Bethlehem. His tomb was discovered several years ago.

ESCAPE TO EGYPT

Just before this massacre God warned Joseph to take his family to Egypt. The Coptic Church has designated many sacred sites where the holy family is supposed to have stayed. None of these sites are authentic. It is most likely that Joseph would have stayed near the border between Egypt and Canaan. In any case they were there only a few weeks for when Herod died the angel instructed Joseph to return to Israel. He chose to travel to his original home in Nazareth. Israeli archaeologists have recently excavated in Nazareth. They uncovered a small house that is not likely to have been the house of Joseph, but it would have been typical of it. They estimate there were probably only about 50 houses in Nazareth at the time Jesus lived there. Everyone would have known of the circumstances surrounding His birth, and He would have been the subject of many sneering remarks about the circumstances of His birth. He "was in all points tempted as we are, yet without sin" (Heb. 4:15).

All Jews were required to go to the temple in Jerusalem every year and no doubt Joseph would have taken Jesus and Mary with him, but the Bible records the visit there when Jesus became 12 years of age. This was probably when He participated in His Bar Mitzvah ceremony after which He was recognized as a child of the law.

THE BAPTISM OF JESUS

For the next 18 years, Jesus toiled patiently as a carpenter. He who by the Word of His mouth had created stars and planets meticulously built houses and reclining couches.

Then tidings came from the River Jordan of a call to repentance by His relative John the Baptist, and Jesus recognized His call to action. Leaving aside His chisel and bidding farewell to His mother, brothers, and sisters, He made the journey to Jericho. John shrank from the request to baptize one with a sinless character but Jesus answered and said to him, "Permit it to be so now, for thus it is fitting for us to fulfill all righteousness" (Matt. 3:15).

After His baptism, "the heavens were opened to Him, and He saw the Spirit of God descending like a dove and

▲ *The shore of the Sea of Galilee, also known as Lake of Genhesaret or Lake Tiberias.*

alighting upon Him. And suddenly a voice came from heaven, saying, "This is My beloved Son, in whom I am well pleased" (Matt. 3:16,17).

"Then Jesus was led up by the Spirit into the wilderness to be tempted by the devil. And when He had fasted forty days and forty nights, afterward He was hungry" (Matt. 4:1–2), "and was with the wild beasts"(Mark 1:13).

A few miles south of Jericho on the north-west shore of the Dead Sea was the Essene settlement of Qumran, near which the Dead Sea scrolls were found. Among the hills behind this settlement would have been a likely place for Jesus to stay. I have wandered among these hills and seen many Ibex. A few years ago the residents of the kibbutz at En Gedi were alarmed when a leopardess and her cub took up residence on the kibbutz lawn. (See Appendix 3.)

Jesus was emaciated and hungry when the devil, pretending to be concerned with His welfare, appeared to Him and said, "If You are the Son of God, command that these stones become bread" (Matt. 4:3).

In this area are many rounded stones resembling loaves of Jewish bread lying on the ground. But hungry as He was, Jesus resisted the temptation. He would not respond to the insinuation that He was not the Son of God. Two more temptations followed but Jesus maintained His divine integrity. At the conclusion of the ordeal, "angels came and ministered to Him" (Matt. 4:11).

Jesus then returned to the river Jordan. As He approached, John the Baptist pointed to Him and said,

"Behold the Lamb of God!" (John 1:36). Like the rest of Israel, John would have been expecting a Messiah who would drive out the Romans and lead Israel to military victories. He could not have understood the significance of the statement he made, but in reality he was announcing a great truth. Jesus was "the Lamb slain from the foundation of the world" (Rev. 13:8). Sin did not take God by surprise. He foresaw the terrible emergency and made provision for it. Father and Son agreed to make the supreme sacrifice which alone could cope with the disaster. "For God so loved the world that He gave His only begotten Son, that whoever believes in Him should not perish but have everlasting life" (John 3:16).

NEW DISCIPLES

Jesus then chose five of John's disciples, Andrew and Simon whom Jesus called kephas, a Hebrew word meaning rock. Later, when the gospels were written he was referred to as Petros, the Greek word for rock. He also called Philip, Nathanael, and the youthful John.

Jesus then led His five new disciples on the arduous three-day journey walking to Cana of Galilee, a village not far from Nazareth. With divine insight Jesus must have known there was a wedding in progress. His mother was there. There is no mention of Joseph who apparently died before this.

Weddings usually lasted several days; they still do in many eastern countries, and the preferred drink was wine.

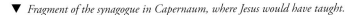

Ruins from the great Synagogue in Capernaum, Israel. ▶

▼ *Fragment of the synagogue in Capernaum, where Jesus would have taught.*

There were three types of wine, as there are in Bible lands today. There was the fresh grape juice called wine in the Bible, alcoholic wine, and a drink called dibbis which was grape juice boiled until it became a thick syrup. Water could be added to reconstitute it as non-alcoholic wine. It is apparent that alcoholic wine was available to guests because some of them were drunk. No doubt dibbis was also available, but as this all happened about November there would have been no fresh grape juice. When the master of ceremonies tasted the wine which Jesus had miraculously provided he said to the bridegroom, "You have kept the good wine until now!" (verse 10). This seems to infer that Jesus had provided fresh grape juice. This would be consistent with the counsel God gave in Proverbs 23:31, "Do not look on the wine when it is red, when it sparkles in the cup."

We do not have any record of Jesus' activity for the next four months. He and His family and disciples went down to Capernaum on the lake of Galilee. His family soon returned to Nazareth. Jesus probably remained in the home of Peter recuperating from His fast.

CONFRONTATION OF THE TEMPLE

April next year Jesus and His small band went to Jerusalem for the Passover week. Jesus was appalled at the trading going on inside the temple precincts. Worshipers had to purchase animals and birds for their sacrifices and the greedy priests were taking advantage of the opportunity for financial gain by allowing sales to take place within the temple area. Offerings could only be made in temple currency, and money changers were charging high exchange rates for those coming from foreign countries. Exercising His divine authority Jesus sternly said, "Take these things away! Do not make My Father's house a house of merchandise!" Greedy traders and crafty priests fled in terror.

There were some who had deplored the abuse of the temple and were impressed with Jesus' air of authority. One was Nicodemus, a member of the ruling Sanhedrin. He wanted to know more about this powerful rabbi. Waiting till the darkness of night concealed his movements, he went across the brook Kedron to the foot of the Mount of Olives in search of Jesus. He no doubt expected Jesus to feel honored by his visit, but instead was startled when Jesus abruptly told him, "unless one is born again, he cannot see the kingdom of God" (John 3:3). Nicodemus was alarmed at the prospect that he, an honored member of the Sanhedrin, may not even see the kingdom of God, but he never forgot the lesson. When Jesus died on the cross he boldly assisted in His burial.

WOMAN AT THE WELL

From Jerusalem Jesus decided to return to Galilee. The usual route was to descend to Jericho and then follow the Jordan Valley, but the more direct route was through Samaria. Most Jews shunned this route because they had to travel across two deep gorges and then pass through the

territory of the hated Samaritans, but Jesus "needed to go through Samaria" (John 4:4). His divine insight told Him there was a woman there who would respond to His message.

It was noon when He and His disciples arrived at Jacob's well and the disciples went into the nearby village to buy food. While Jesus waited at the well, a Samaritan woman approached and seeming oblivious of Jesus' presence lowered the water pot from her head. She was startled when Jesus asked her for a drink. That was a request that no one in the east would refuse but the woman was surprised that Jesus, a Jew, would speak to her, a Samaritan. Jesus told her that He could give her living water. She expressed her desire to have this water that would relieve her of the bother of coming to the well to draw. But Jesus wanted to reach her heart with His message. "Go call your husband," He said. That was embarrassing. A discussion about her private life was the last thing she wanted. She tried to dismiss the matter by saying, "I have no husband." Looking her firmly in the eyes, Jesus startled her by saying, "you have had five husbands, and the one whom you now have is not your husband" (verse 38).

Some Bible commentators have deplored this woman's promiscuity, but she had many commendable qualities. She was obviously intelligent and well spoken. She was spiritually minded and well read in the Scriptures. Also, she had not had five husbands because she was promiscuous; women did not divorce their husbands. It is likely these husbands had divorced her because she was infertile. That would also explain why she came to the well at midday instead of early morning as most women did. She came there at midday to avoid the women who scorned and ridiculed her because she was infertile. Remember how Hagar scorned Sarah and Peninnah treated Hannah with contempt because of their infertility.

This mistreated Samaritan woman was so excited about her discovery that she forgot her water pot and hastened back to her village to tell the men (not the women) that she had found the Messiah. She was the only person to whom Jesus ever made the claim to be the Messiah.

BETHESDA TO CAPERNAUM

From Samaria, Jesus walked further north to Cana where He healed the nobleman's son and then made the arduous walk back to Jerusalem. Here He performed His first miracle on the Sabbath in the pool of Bethesda. This is one of the very few genuine sites in the life of Jesus. The Bible says there was a pool with five arches (John 5:2), and the arches are still there. Here was a man who had been lame for 38 years. Jesus told him to take up his bedroll and walk. The man did not ask how he could walk while he was in that condition. There was something about Jesus that inspired him with confidence. He stood to his feet and walked. But the Jews were not impressed. They accused the man of carrying a burden on the Sabbath day. They then arraigned Jesus before the Sanhedrin, the governing body of the Jews at that time. Jesus' lengthy defense is recorded in John chapter 5. He solemnly warned them that "the hour is coming in which all who are in the graves will hear His voice and come forth-those who have done good, to the resurrection of life, and those who have done evil, to the resurrection of condemnation" (John 5:28–29).

Then it was back to Nazareth. Jesus was invited to read from the Scriptures, and He chose a passage in Isaiah which predicted the work of the expected Messiah, concluding by saying, "Today this Scripture is fulfilled in your hearing."

Ruins of Byzantine church near St. Anne Church and pool of Bethesda in Jerusalem. ▶

◀ *The James Ossuary is a 2,000-year old limestone box used for containing the bones of the dead. It is significant because this controversial archaeological evidence suggests that there was a historical person named Jesus whose father was Joseph and brother was James as written in the Bible and in the works of Jewish historian Josephus.*

This was Jesus, the son of Joseph. He had grown up in their village. That He was now claiming to be the Messiah was more than they could tolerate. They hustled him to the edge of a cliff intending to hurl Him to His death, but He miraculously disappeared from their sight and departed.

We next read of Jesus in Capernaum at the north end of the Lake of Galilee. Until now His little group of disciples had been part-time followers. Now He called them to full-time discipleship.

Already a crowd was gathering to hear Jesus speak, so He borrowed a small boat belonging to Peter and from this He spoke to the crowd. What a scene was this for angels to behold. The Majesty of heaven rocked to and fro by the waters of the lake, speaking the words of life to the expectant throng.

When His discourse was ended, Jesus ordered Peter to get in the boat, to push out from the shore, and let down his nets to catch some fish. Peter was condescending; all fishing on the clear waters of the lake was done during the dark hours of night when the fish could not so readily see the nets. Jesus had been a carpenter. He could not be expected to know about fishing, but Peter agreed. He was astonished to gather a huge haul of fish. This was a miracle that could appeal to a fisherman. Peter recognized in Jesus the attributes of divinity; he was in great awe. Casting himself at Jesus' feet he exclaimed, "Depart from me, for I am a sinful man, O Lord!" (Luke 5:8). Jesus bade the four fishermen to leave their nets and follow Him full time. They were privileged to see Jesus heal the sick, open the eyes of the blind, cleanse the lepers, and raise the dead to life.

SERIES OF EVENTS

At Capernaum lived a Levitical priest who had degenerated so far as to become a tax collector for the Roman government. He had heard the words of life falling from Jesus' lips and seen His miracles. Within his soul there was a longing for something better but he could not expect Jesus to help him. He was astonished one day when Jesus paused beside his tax collecting table and said to him, "follow me." Without a moment's hesitation, he informed his family of his intentions and followed Jesus. He was Levi Matthew who later wrote the first of the gospels.

The Jews were looking for a Messiah who would marshal the armies of Israel, drive out the hated Romans, and make Israel a great nation. The time had come for Jesus to spell out the nature of the kingdom He had come to establish. He prayed on a hillside all night and with the dawn of day He descended to where the disciples had been sleeping. Beside the six disciples He already had, He called six others, including Judas, and laying His hands on their heads He ordained them as His twelve chosen disciples who would one day be responsible for preaching His message to the entire known world. Then He led the disciples, and the expectant crowd that had gathered, up the hill where He spoke to them the Sermon on the Mount.

From then on there was a series of miracles and discourses that brought peace and joy to the people, but which aroused the hostility of priests and rulers who were more concerned with ceremonial purity than sincerity of heart. It culminated, after three years of self-sacrificing ministry in His final visit to Jerusalem. He warned the disciples of His impending betrayal and death, but as it did not conform to their concept of the Messiah they dismissed it from their minds.

FINAL DAYS

That last week of Jesus' life was fraught with drama. On Saturday night, He attended the feast in the house of Simon whom He had cured of leprosy. It was there that Mary Magdalene, out of whom Jesus had expelled seven demons, anointed His feet with her expensive perfume and wiped His feet with her tears.

The next day, Jesus rode in triumph into Jerusalem, and the disciples were elated. Their hopes were being fulfilled. The crowds were accepting Him as the long hoped for Messiah, but then followed three days of heated opposition from priests and Pharisees. Jesus met all their accusations with quotations from the Scriptures and parables that illustrated His teaching. He left the temple for the last time after uttering the fateful words, "Look, your house is left to you desolate." Without the presence of divinity the temple was nothing more than a hollow shell.

Even the disciples were in awe. Four of them followed Him to the crest of the Mount of Olives and when He was seated they asked Him, "What will be the sign of Your coming, and of the end of the world?" (Matt. 24:3). They assumed that the desolation of their temple must be at the end of the world.

Jesus unfolded to them the events leading up to the conquest of Jerusalem and the demolition of the temple by the Romans in 70 AD, then on to events preceding the second coming of Christ.

The Passover week was about to begin, and on the Thursday night Jesus observed the ceremony with His disciples. At this time He instituted the communion service with its broken bread symbolizing His crucified body, and the wine which symbolized His spilt blood. It was then that Judas left the upper room and made his way to the priests where he arranged to betray Jesus for 30 pieces of silver.

Jesus and His disciples then made their way over the brook Kedron to the foot of the Mount of Olives where He prayed that the cup of suffering might pass from Him. But there was only one way sinful humanity could ever find acceptance with God, and that was by the death of the sinless Son of God.

JESUS ROSE TO MEET HIS FATE.

Judas led the murderous throng that arrested Jesus, and they led Him to the palace of Annas the father-in-law of the presiding high priest. Annas was unable to extract anything from Jesus that would procure His condemnation and sent Him on to

Caiaphas, the ruling high priest at that time.

Recently, archaeologists in Jerusalem opened a tomb in the Kedron Valley and found an ossuary on which was inscribed the name Kaiaphas. They believe it contained the bones of the high priest who presided over Jesus' trial. It is now in the Israel Museum.

After a mock trial at which false witnesses could not agree, Caipahas at last in desperation rose from his seat and demanded that Jesus tell them plainly if He was the Son of God. To this demand Jesus could not remain silent. "I say to you, hereafter you will see the Son of Man sitting at the right hand of the Power, and coming on the clouds of heaven" (Matt. 26:64).

It was all they needed. Caiaphas tore his robe in mock horror, thereby bringing on himself the condemnation of God. Moses had specifically written that the high priest was not to tear his robes.

Christ was then subjected to inhuman abuse and cruelty. Ruthless men struck Him on the cheeks, others spat in His face. The Creator patiently submitted to all this abuse with deepest serenity.

When the full Sanhedrin was assembled, they unanimously condemned Jesus to death, but the Jews were under Roman rule and were not authorized to put anyone to death. At about six in the morning, they led Him to Pilate, the Roman governor at that time.

Pilate could find no cause of guilt and sent Him to Herod who was in Jerusalem at that time. Even Herod dared not condemn an innocent man and sent him back to Pilate. The latter could still not find any reason to condemn Jesus, but because of the clamor of the priests and people he washed his hands of the case, and after Jesus was mercilessly flogged he delivered Him to be crucified.

Jesus was then taken to "a place called Golgotha, that is to say, Place of a Skull" (Matt. 27:33). From Pilate's judgment hall, Jesus would have been hustled along the narrow city road to the Sheep Gate where Arab shepherds still trade their sheep and goats. Less than 100 meters beyond this gate is a cliff face. Caves in the face of this cliff present the appearance of a huge skull, and the place is known as Gordon's Calvary. Here at the foot of the cliff Jesus was laid on the cross and the cruel spikes were driven through His

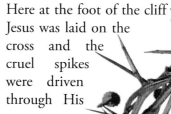

▲ *Garden Tomb in Jerusalem, one of two sites proposed as the place of Jesus' burial.*

quivering flesh. The only cry that escaped His lips was, "Father, forgive them, for they do not know what they do" (Luke 23:34).

The cross was then lifted by strong men and thrust into the hole prepared for it. This caused agonizing pain to Jesus as the weight of His body would have torn gaping holes in His hands.

During these hours of suffering, Jesus did not lose sight of those He came to save. Seeing His aged mother standing in front of His cross, and His young disciple John nearby, He committed His mother to John's care.

At midday, a mysterious darkness fell on the scene. Two thieves had been crucified with Jesus. At first they both scoffed at Jesus, but as time went by one of the thieves began to think of the retribution awaiting him in the afterlife. Turning his head to Jesus, he uttered a despairing cry, "Lord, remember me when You come into Your kingdom." Immediately, Jesus responded, "Assuredly, I say to you, today you will be with Me in Paradise" (Luke 21:42,43).

After six agonizing hours, Jesus felt His heart rupture and cried out, "Father, 'into Your hands I commit My spirit.'" He then bowed His head and died.

THE END BECOMES THE BEGINNING

The disciples were crushed. Their hopes were extinguished. In profound grief they watched as Joseph and Nicodemus placed the body of Jesus in a tomb. The next day a large round stone was rolled against the entrance of the tomb, which was then sealed with the Roman seal to ensure that no unauthorized person could interfere with the body of Jesus. But no heavy stone or Roman seal could keep the Son of God in the tomb. On Sunday morning, an angel came and rolled away the stone and the Son of God came forth.

Subsequently, Jesus appeared to His disciples in the upper room, to two believers as they walked to Emmaus, again to the disciples when doubting Thomas was present, to five of the disciples as they fished by the sea, to 500 believers on a hill in Galilee, and finally to His disciples in Jerusalem. There were many witnesses to His resurrection. From there He led them over the hill to the region of Bethany where He ascended to heaven. The disciples watched in wonder as He rose from among them and was escorted by a cloud of angels to the throne of God His Father.

But the disciples were not left to mourn His departure. As He disappeared from their sight, two angels appeared beside them and spoke the comforting words, "This same Jesus, who was taken up from you into heaven, will so come in like manner as you saw Him go into heaven" (Acts 1:11).

Incredible! The Savior walked this earth for 33 years, unrecognized and dishonored, but one day soon He will return as "KING OF KINGS AND LORD OF LORDS" (Rev. 19:16). And the good news is that we can be "caught up together with them in the clouds to meet the Lord in the air. And thus we shall always be with the Lord" (1 Thess. 4:16–17)!

APPENDIX 1

Images are taken from The Complete Works of Flavius Josephus, the Jewish Historian (J.&E. Tallis London Edinburgh& Dublin).

TABERNACLE LIFE

High Priest in his Robes.

High Priest on the Day of Expiation.

Common Priest.

Altar of Incense.

Ark of the Covenant.

Brazen Altar of the Burnt Sacrifice.

Table of Shew Bread.

Levites.

The Tabernacle – A Moveable Sanctuary
(Exodus 25–29)

The Golden Candlestick.

Setting Up the Tabernacle.

APPENDIX 2

A description of Solomon's Temple from Newton's Revised History of Ancient Kingdoms.

SOLOMON'S TEMPLE

b f e d c b
U X
Q M N R
k k
H D C I
z z
A B s
m n
r
F E
u
L K

1 100 200 300

T S
Z Y
a a

Diagram of Solomon's Temple
(Ezekiel 40:5–23)

ABCD	The *Separate Place* where the temple was built
ABEF	The *Priests' Court*
G	The Altar
DHLKICEFD	A pavement surrounding three sides of the *Priests' Court* and on which stood the buildings for the priests and the adjoining cloisters below them
MNOP	The *People's Court*
MQTSRN	The pavement surrounding three sides of the *People's Court* on which stood the buildings for the people with the cloisters below them
UXYZ	The *Mountain of the House*
aabb	A wall enclosing the entire temple complex
c	The gate called Shallecheth
d	The gate called Parbar
ef	The two gates called Asuppim
g	The east gate of the *People's Court* called the *King's Gate*
hh	The north and south gates of the *People's Court*
iiii &c.	The 30 rooms over the cloisters of the *People's Court* where the priests ate the sacrifices
kkkk	The four small courts serving for staircases and kitchens for the people
l	The eastern gate of the *Priests' Court* above which the Sanhedrin met
m	The southern gate of the *Priests' Court*
n	The northern gate of the *Priests' Court* where the sacrifices were prepared
opqrst	The buildings above the cloisters for the priests. These were six large subdivided rooms on each storey
op	The rooms for the high priest and his deputy, the Sagan
q	The room for the overseers of the sanctuary and treasury
r	The room for the overseers of the altar and the sacrifice
st	The rooms for the princes of the 24 courses of priests
uu	The two courts containing the staircases and the kitchens for the priests
x	The house or temple (along with the treasure rooms "y" and the buildings "zz" on each side of the *Separate Place*).

APPENDIX 3

IN THE YEAR 1947, ONE OF THE GREATEST archaeological discoveries of the twentieth century was made in the arid wilderness by the shores of the Dead Sea in Israel. The discovery of the Dead Sea scrolls was made, not by skilled archaeologists, but by Arab Bedouins who tended their flocks in the region. The find was to make sensational headlines in newspapers and scholarly journals around the world, and the results would influence the views of scholars and theologians for decades to come.

Muhammad Adh-Dhib was a boy belonging to the Ta'amireh tribe of Arab Bedouin who lived between Bethlehem and the Dead Sea, an area referred to in the Bible as the Wilderness of Judea (Matt. 3:1). In the day Muhammad cared for his father's goats, searching for the scarce blades of grass that grew between the barren rocks in this area. At night he sat by the tribal campfire listening to the elders discuss such important matters as the price of sheep in the Bethlehem bazaar, the possibility of taking a fourth wife, or the progress of the fighting that was disturbing the tranquility of their land at that time.

One day as Muhammad minded his goats, he became aware that one of them was missing. Apparently, unnoticed by the lad, it had strayed from the flock and so he went to hunt for it. After a fruitless search, the boy wearily threw himself onto the stony ground in the shade of an overhanging crag. As his eyes wandered listlessly over the glaring rocks, he noticed a rather strange hole in the rock face. The hole was a little bigger than a man's head and seemed to be the entrance to one of the many caves in the area.

Driven by curiosity, the Bedouin youth pulled himself up to the hole and peered in. His eyes had hardly become accustomed to the gloom when he had to release his grip and drop to the ground, but what he had seen in those few moments made him catch his breath in amazement. On the floor of the cave were a number of cylindrical objects standing in rows. He waited no longer. His goat forgotten, Muhammad sped from the place, seeking to put as much distance as possible between him and this djinni-ridden cave, for what but desert spirits would inhabit such a place?

That night, Muhammad told his secret to an older boy who was less superstitious. The next day the two boys went to the cave

The Psalms scroll, one of the 972 texts from the Hebrew Bible ▼

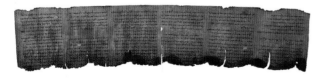

▲ *The Shrine of the Book in Jerusalem was constructed to resemble the lid of the clay jars that held the scrolls.*

and, emboldened by each other's presence, squeezed through the hole and dropped inside. It was just as the younger boy had described. Rows of jars stood on each side of the cave, and in the center lay debris that had fallen from the roof.

The older boy lifted the lid of one of the tall slender jars, and peering inside, found it empty, and so with another. In the third jar, however, they found a bundle of old rags, and under these, two more bundles. If they had hoped for the glitter of gold or precious stones, they were sorely disappointed. Drawing aside the musty cloth, all they could find were some rolls of old leather. The boys were disgusted at their find and, stuffing some of the rolls beneath their belts, they squeezed their way out of the hole and returned to their camp. Little did they realize that just one of these rolls would later be sold in America for a quarter of a million dollars.

That night they unrolled one of the leather bundles and found that it stretched from one side of the tent to the other. On it was some writing, which they could not read. Next time the men of the tribe went to Bethlehem for trading, they took the rolls with them and showed them to the owner of a store there. The trader's name was Kando, who thought the scrolls might have some value.

The Scrolls to Jerusalem

Next time Kando went to Jerusalem, he took the scrolls with him and showed them to his spiritual adviser, Bishop Samuel of the Syrian convent of Saint Mark. It so happened that the man had studied ancient manuscripts in the course of his training and had often dreamed of finding such a scroll. He offered to buy the scroll, but Kando said there were more and it would be better to deal with the whole lot. To this the Bishop agreed, and Kando went his way with a promise to return. The date was April 1947.

It was not until July that Kando returned with the Bedouin. Bishop Samuel was expecting them. All morning he waited in a fever of anticipation, but he waited in vain. He went to lunch with the other priests, fearing that they had taken their treasure elsewhere. But as they dined, he happened to overhear Father Gelph mention an incident that had occurred earlier in the morning. What he heard sent his teaspoon clattering to the saucer. "You did what?" he demanded. "I sent them away. They had some filthy scrolls wrapped in sticky linen and they wanted to see your Grace. But I was firm with them, I knew your Grace would not want those smelly old things in our monastery." The Bishop leapt from his chair and made an undignified exit, leaving a table of bewildered priests.

Another appointment was made, and a few weeks later, on August 5, Kando arrived with two Bedouin, including the boy who had discovered the cave. From an old bag Kando produced five ancient scrolls. Some hard bargaining ensued, and to each offer Kando scornfully clicked his

Jar that the Dead Sea Scrolls were found in.

tongue in refusal. At last the Bishop opened his drawer and took out a roll of Jordanian Dinars.

"This is all the money I have in the world. I can offer no more," he said with finality. Kando snapped up the money, and with expert fingers quickly counted it — sixty odd dinars (about 250 American dollars). Kando shrugged his shoulders and then pushed the scrolls across the table to the Bishop. "We hope they bring your Grace happiness," he said politely, and the bishop was left alone with the scrolls.

During the next few weeks, Bishop Samuel showed his acquisition to a number of scholars and told his story, but the usual response was one of sympathy that he had wasted his valuable dinars. The Bedouin were always "finding things" they assured him and there was no chance of these scrolls being genuine. But the Bishop was not discouraged.

The political situation continued to throw the country into turmoil and on November 29, the United Nations General Assembly recommended the partition of Palestine into an Arab and Israeli state. Open hostilities broke out making it dangerous to move around Jerusalem.

In January 1948, a friend of the Bishop arranged a meeting with a noted Hebrew scholar, Professor Sukenik of the Hebrew University. The professor borrowed the scrolls for a week and then pronounced them very ancient and offered to buy them. But no price was agreed upon and the deal was not finalized.

The Bishop next contacted the American Schools of Oriental Research and was put in touch with Doctor John Trever, a noted Hebrew scholar and a skilled photographer. Doctor Trever identified them as being very old and photographed them and discovered that one of the scrolls was an ancient copy of the book of Isaiah. He dispatched his photos by airmail to Professor Albright of America's John

Hopkins University, the world's foremost authority on Palestinian archaeology. On March 15, a telegram was received, "My heartiest congratulations on the greatest discovery of modern times," it read. "I should prefer a date around 100 BC."

100 BC? That would make it 1000 years older than any known manuscript of the Old Testament. But the drama was not yet over.

Because of the hostilities, Doctor Trever advised the Bishop to take such treasure out of the country lest it be destroyed in the fighting. The Metropolitan took his advice and escaped to the United States where he finally sold it to a representative of the Israeli government. It was later returned to Israel and is now housed in the Shrine of the Book at the Hebrew Museum.

A Beduin's Discovery

Now that the Bedouin had got the smell of dinars, goats were well nigh forgotten in a frantic search for caves and scrolls. One night, as the men sat around the campfire discussing the latest finds, one old man suddenly remembered an incident that had occurred many years before. He had been out shooting partridge when he felled a bird on the wing. On hitting the ground, the partridge had flapped its way along a ridge and then disappeared into a hole in the side of a cliff. When the Bedouin entered the hole to retrieve the bird, he had found himself in a cave, "and come to think of it, there were some broken jars in the cave!" "Where is it?" his eager listeners chorused. Next day the old man led them to the cave, and sure enough, they found more scrolls, which were by now selling for $4 per square centimeter.

This cave became known as "the cave of the wounded partridge," and it is right beside the ruins of an old settlement at a place called Khirbet Qumran. Here, a Jewish sect of ascetics known as the Essenes may have lived, and here they copied books of the Bible. Many coins were found in the excavations, and the latest date on these coins was AD 68 when the building may have been destroyed by fire. Apparently, the occupants had lived here until the Roman armies marched on Jerusalem, and fearing that the Romans would kill them, they had hastily hidden their precious

▲ *Dead Sea Cave number 4 where many fragments of scrolls were found.*

▲ *The remains of the west wing of the main building at Qumran, located one kilometer inland from the northwest shore of the Dead Sea.*

scrolls in caves and fled to Jerusalem, which was conquered and destroyed by the Romans in AD 70. The occupants had most likely perished in the war and had never returned to their settlement, and the scrolls remained hidden until 1947. Altogether, 11 caves containing scrolls were found.

The importance of the scrolls lay not in their ancient paper, or in the old script that was used, but in their contents. Here were copies of the Bible far older than any that had ever been found. What would be written there? Would the scholars find that our present Bible is only a garbled edition of the original writings? With eager anticipation they went to work, comparing the wording of these ancient manuscripts with the wording of the Bible we use today.

Only Minor Discrepencies

To be sure, there were discrepancies. For instance, in the King James Version (known as the KJV) in Isaiah 6:3, an angel is recorded as saying, "Holy, holy, holy, is the LORD of hosts." In the Dead Sea Scroll it reads, "Holy, holy, is the LORD of Hosts." One less "holy." In the KJV, there are several places where it says "LORD" where the scrolls say "God." In 1 Samuel 1:24, the KJV says that Hannah took Samuel up to the tabernacle "with three bullocks." The scrolls say that she took him up "with a bullock of three years." So there are discrepancies, but extensive examination showed that there was nothing that changed the essential meaning of the text.

So those who read the Old Testament today can have the assurance that what they are reading is what the prophets wrote thousands of years ago. Three thousand years ago David had written, "The words of the LORD are pure words... thou shalt preserve them from this generation for ever" (Ps. 12:6–7).

Scholars are still studying these scrolls, and in 2006 there was a convention of Dead Sea Scroll scholars to discuss the latest developments. One scholar read a paper in which he said that he had studied a scroll that contained Psalm 145 and it had all 22 verses. The missing verse was verse 14, which read, "God is faithful and glorious in all his deeds."

In the meantime many more ancient manuscripts have come to light, and by comparing these ancient documents scholars have been able to publish translations of the Bible which are not only in modern English, but which must be very close to the original text. As with the Old Testament, there may still be some doubt about the precise wording of some texts, and there may be variations in the way certain Hebrew or Greek words should be translated.

As there were no punctuation marks used by the original Bible writers (in fact the New Testament writers who wrote in the Greek language did not even leave gaps between words), the punctuation marks in English Bibles may, in some cases, be in the wrong position. But there need be no doubt about the general accuracy and truth of the Bible. There are many texts relating to any vital topic in the Bible and careful comparison of all related texts on any given subject will enable sincere seekers of truth to arrive at the right conclusions.

APPENDIX 4

Tables are taken from The Complete Works of Flavius Josephus, the Jewish Historian.

TABLE I

COMPARATIVE VIEW OF THE LIVES OF THE PATIARCHS

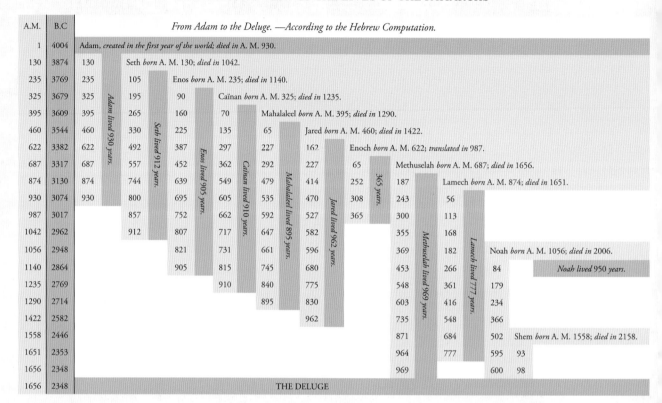

From Adam to the Deluge. —According to the Hebrew Computation.

A.M.	B.C										
1	4004	Adam, *created in the first year of the world; died in A. M. 930.*
130	3874	130	Seth *born* A. M. 130; *died in* 1042.
235	3769	235	105	Enos *born* A. M. 235; *died in* 1140.
325	3679	325	195	90	Caïnan *born* A. M. 325; *died in* 1235.
395	3609	395	265	160	70	Mahalaleel *born* A. M. 395; *died in* 1290.
460	3544	460	330	225	135	65	Jared *born* A. M. 460; *died in* 1422.
622	3382	622	492	387	297	227	162	Enoch *born* A. M. 622; *translated in* 987.
687	3317	687	557	452	362	292	227	65	Methuselah *born* A. M. 687; *died in* 1656.
874	3130	874	744	639	549	479	414	252	187	Lamech *born* A. M. 874; *died in* 1651.
930	3074	930	800	695	605	535	470	308	243	56
987	3017		857	752	662	592	527	365	300	113
1042	2962		912	807	717	647	582		355	168
1056	2948			821	731	661	596		369	182	Noah *born* A. M. 1056; *died in* 2006.
1140	2864			905	815	745	680		453	266	84	Noah lived 950 years.
1235	2769				910	840	775		548	361	179
1290	2714					895	830		603	416	234
1422	2582						962		735	548	366
1558	2446								871	684	502	Shem *born* A. M. 1558; *died in* 2158.
1651	2353								964	777	595	93
1656	2348								969		600	98
1656	2348	THE DELUGE

Adam lived 930 years. — Seth lived 912 years. — Enos lived 905 years. — Caïnan lived 910 years. — Mahalaleel lived 895 years. — Jared lived 962 years. — 365 years. — Methuselah lived 969 years. — Lamech lived 777 years.

TABLE II

CHRONOLOGICAL TABLE, FROM CREATION TO THE BIRTH OF OUR LORD

According to the Supputations of three celebrated Writers.	USHER. Following the Hebrew.				JOSEPHUS.				PEZRON. Following the Septuagint.			
	1. Year of the World.	2. Year of the Flood.	3. Year before Christ.	4. Years of the Interval.	1. Year of the World.	2. Year of the Flood.	3. Year before Christ.	4. Years of the Interval.	1. Year of the World.	2. Year of the Flood.	3. Year before Christ.	4. Years of the Interval.
1. Creation	0	—	4004	—	0	—	4658	—	1	—	5873	—
2. Deluge	1656	—	2348	1656	1556	—	3102	1556	2256	—	3617	2256
3. Vocation of Abraham	2083	427	1921	427	2523	976	2135	967	3513	1257	2360	1257
4. Exodus of Israel	2513	857	1491	430	2953	1397	1705	430	3943	1687	1930	430
Death of Moses	[2553]	—	—	—	[2993]	—	—	—	—	—	—	—
5. Foundation of the Temple	2992	1336	1012	479	3545	1989	1113	592	4816	2560	1057	873
Captivity	3397	1741	607	—	—	—	—	—	[5268]	3012	605	452
6. Temple burned	3416	1760	588	424	4015	2459	643	470	5287	3031	586	[19]
First Edict, by Cyrus	3468	—	—	—	4085	—	—	[70]	[5337]	3081	536	69
Second Edict, by Darius Hystaspis	3486	—	—	[70]	—	—	—	—	[5351]	3095	520	14
7. Nativity of our Lord	4004	2348	0	588	4658	3102	0	643	5873	3617	1	522
Total number of Years	—	—	—	4004	—	—	—	4658	—	—	—	5873

TABLE III

TABLE OF THE JEWISH WEIGHTS, MEASURES, &c. AND PARTICULARLY THOSE MENTIONED IN JOSEPHUS' WORK.

Of the Jewish Measures of Length.

	Inches	Feet.	Inches.
Cubit, the standard	21	1	9
Zereth, or large span	10.5	1	0
Small span	7	0	0
Palm, or hand's breath	3.5	0	0
Inch, or thumb's breadth	1.16	0	0
Digit, or finger's breadth	.875	0	0
Orgyia, or fathom	84	7	0
Ezekiel's Canneh, or reed	126	10	6
Arabian Canneh, or pole	168	14	0
Schænus line, or chain	1680	140	0
Sabbath-day's journey	42000	3500	0
Jewish mile	84000	7000	0
Stadium, or furlong	8400	700	0
Parasang	252000	21000	0

Of the Jewish Weights and Coins.

	£.	s.	d.
Statur, Silus, or shekel of the sanctuary, the standard	0	2	6
Tyrian Coin, equal to the shekel	0	2	6
Bekah, half of the shekel	0	1	3
Drachma Attica, one fourth	0	0	7.5
Drachma Alexandrina, or Darchmon, or Adarchmon, one half	0	1	3
Gerah, or Obulus, one-twentieth	0	0	1.5
Maneh, Mna—100 shekels in weight—21900 grains Troy. Maneh, Mna, or Mina, as a coin—60 shekels	7	10	0
Talent of silver—300 shekels	375	0	0
Drachma of gold, not more than	0	1	1
Shekel of gold, not more than	0	4	4
Daric of gold	1	0	4
Talent of gold, not more than	648	0	0

Of the Jewish Measures of Capacity.

	Cub. Inches	Pints or Pounds.
Bath, or Epha	807,274	27.83
Corus, or Chomer	8072.74	278.3
Seah, or Saton	269.091	9.266
Ditto, according to Josephus	828.28	28.3
Hin	134.54	4.4633
Ditto, according to Josephus	414.12	14.3
Omer, ot Asseron	80.727	2.78
Cab	44.859	1.544
Log	11.21	.39
Metretes, or Syrian firkin	207	7.125

Table of Jewish Months in Josephus and others, with the Syro-Macedonian Names Josephus gives them, and the Names of the Julian or Roman Months corresponding to them.

Hebrew Names.	Syro-Macedonian Names.	Roman Names
1. Nisan	Xanthicus	March and April
2. Jyar	Artemisius	April and May
3. Sivan	Dæsius	May and June
4. Tamuz	Panemus	June and July
5. Ab	Lous	July and August
6. Elul	Gorpiæus	August and September
7. Tisri	Hyperbertæi	September and October
8. Marhesvan	Dius	October and November
9. Casleu	Appeliæus	November and December
10. Tebeth	Audinæus	December and January
11. Shebat	Peritius	January and February
12. Adar	Dystrus	February and March

13. Ve Adar, or The second Adar intercalated.

ENDNOTES

CHAPTER 1

1. D. Winton Thomas, editor, *Documents from Old Testament Times* (New York: Harper and Rowe, 1958).
2. Lovett, Tim. Noah's Ark: Thinking Outside the Box; Green Forest, AR: Master Books, 2008. Page 32.

CHAPTER 2

1. C. Leonard Woolley, *The Sumerians* (New York: W.W. Norton, 1965), p. 109–110.
2. Ya'acov Shkolnik, "Moon capital of Mesopotamia," *Eretz* (March 2002): p. 35.
3. Ibid., p. 35.
4. Ibid., p. 135.
5. Flavius Josephus, *Antiquities of the Jews*, 1, VIII, 2.

CHAPTER 3

1. John Ashton and David Down, *Unwrapping the Pharaohs* (Green Forest, AR: Master Books, 2006).
2. Flavius Josephus, *Antiquities of the Jews*, I. VIII. 2.

CHAPTER 4

1. Jack M. Sasson, "The Servant's Tale: How Rebekah Found a Spouse," *Journal of Near Eastern Studies*, vol. 65, no. 4 (October 2006), p. 241–265.
2. Ibid., p. 245.
3. Ibid., p. 245.
4. Ibid., p. 246.
5. Ibid., p. 262.
6. Ibid.

CHAPTER 5

1. Amarna Letter EA288.
2. Amarna Letter EA281.

CHAPTER 6

1. Heinrich Brugsch Bey, *Egypt Under the Pharaohs* (London: J. Murray; New York: Scriber, 1891), p. 158.
2. Herodotus, *Herodotus: The Histories*, translated by Walter Blanco, edited by Walter Blanco and Jennifer Tolbert Roberts (New York: Norton, 1992), p. 160.
3. A. Rosalie David, *The Pyramid Builders of Ancient Egypt* (London; Boston: Routledge & K. Paul, 1986), p. 191.
4. Ibid., p. 192.
5. Ibid., p. 195.
6. Ibid., p. 199.

CHAPTER 7

1. Rudolph Cohen, "The Mysterious MBI People," *Biblical Archaeology Review* (July 1983): p. 16.
2. Ibid., p. 17.
3. Ibid., p. 19.
4. Ibid., p. 25.
5. Ibid., p. 28.
6. Ibid., p. 29.

CHAPTER 8

1. Nelson Glueck, *Rivers in the Desert* (New York: Farrar, Straus and Cudahy, 1959), p. ix.
2. Ibid., p. xi.
3. Ibid., p. 3.
4. Ibid., p. 94.

CHAPTER 9

1. John Garstang and J.B.E. Garstang, *The Story of Jericho* (London: Marshall, Morgan & Scott, 1940), p. 136.
2. Ibid., p. 141.
3. Ibid., p. 142.
4. Kathleen Kenyon, *Digging Up Jericho* (New York: Praeger, 1957), p. 46.
5. Kathleen Kenyon, *Archaeology in the Holy Land* (London: Ernest Benn Limited, 1965), p. 134.
6. Ibid., p. 194–195.
7. Ibid., p. 207.
8. J.B. Pritchard, *Where the Sun Stood Still* (Calabasas, CA: Toucan Pub., 1992), p. 153.
9. Israel Finkelstein, *The Bible Unearthed* (New York: Free Press, 2001), p. 5.

CHAPTER 10

1. Amihai Mazar, *Archaeology of the Land of the Bible* (New York: Doubleday, 1990), p. 331.
2. B. Cobbey Crisler, "The Acoustics and Crowd Capacity of Natural Theaters in Palestine," *Biblical Archaeologist* (December 1976): p. 139.
3. Israel Finkelstein, *Biblical Archaeology Review* (January 1981): p. 34.
4. Ibid.
5. George L. Kelm and Amihai Mazar, *Timna: a Biblical City in the Sorek Valley* (Winona Lake, IN: Eisenbrauns, 1995), p. 61.

CHAPTER 11

1. Yadin Roman, *Eretz* (July 1998).

CHAPTER 12

1. Israel Finkelstein and Neil Asher Silberman, *David and Solomon* (New York: Free Press, 2006), p. 21.
2. Ibid., p. 22.
3. Ibid., p. 80.
4. Ibid., p. 33.
5. Ibid., p. 274.
6. Avraham Biran, *Biblical Dan* (Jerusalem: Israel Exploration Society; Hebrew Union College-Jewish Institute of Religion, 1994), p. 277.
7. Israel Finkelstein, *The Archaeology of the Israelite Settlement* (Jerusalem: Israel Exploration Society, 1988), p. 348.

CHAPTER 13

1. Israel Finkelstein and Neil Asher Silberman, *David and Solomon* (New York: Free Press, 2006), p. 153.
2. Ibid., p. 153.
3. Amihai Mazar, *Archaeology of the Land of the Bible 10,000–586 B.C.E.* (New York: Doubleday, 1990), p. 174.
4. Ibid., p. 208, 214.
5. Israel Finkelstein, *The Archaeology of the Israelite Settlement* (Jerusalem: Israel Exploration Society, 1988), p. 339.
6. Ibid., p. 274.
7. Flavius Josephus, *Antiquities of the Jews*, Book VIII, chapter VI, para. 5.

CHAPTER 14

1. Michael Coogan, *Stories from Ancient Canaan* (Philadelphia, PA: Westminster Press, 1978), p. 79.
2. Ibid., p. 110.
3. Ibid., p. 113.
4. Ibid., p. 109.

CHAPTER 15

1. O.R. Gurney, *The Hittites* (London; Baltimore, MD: Penguin Books, 1952), p. 39.

CHAPTER 16

1. James Maxwell Miller and John Haralson Hayes, *A History of Ancient Israel and Judah* (Louisville, KY: Westminster John Knox Press, 2006), p. 361).
2. James Pritchard, *The Ancient Near East* (Princeton, NJ: Princeton University Press, 1958), p. 206–208.
3. E.A. Speiser and James B. Pritchard, *Ancient Near Eastern Texts Relating to the New Testament*, 3rd ed. (Princeton, NJ: Princeton University Press, 1969), p. 287–288.

CHAPTER 17

1. D. Winton Thomas, *Documents from Old Testament Times* (New York: Harper, 1961), p. 86.
2. Israel Finkelstein, *The Archaeology of the Israelite Settlement* (Jerusalem: Israel Exploration Society, 1988), p. 339–341.
3. Edward Gibbon, *The Decline and Fall of the Roman Empire* (UK: Sadler & Brown, 1967).

CHAPTER 18

1. Geoffrey W. Bromiley, *International Standard Bible Encyclopedia, Vol. 1* (Grand Rapids, MI: W.B. Eerdmans, 1979, 1988), p. 846–847.

CHAPTER 19

1. James W. Watts, editor, *Persia and Torah: The Theory of Imperial Authorization of the Pentateuch* (Atlanta, GA: Society of Biblical Literature, 2001), p. 103.

INDEX

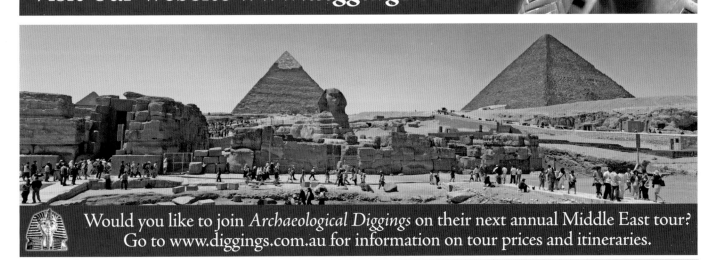
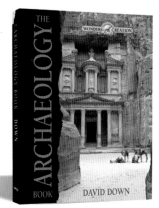

THE CHRONOLOGY
OF THE OLD TESTAMENT

DR. FLOYD NOLEN JONES

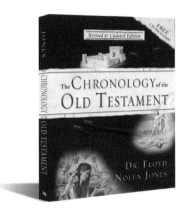

Following Master Books' release and unprecedented sales of Ussher's *The Annals of the World*, the release of this amazing book had to be next. *The Chronology of the Old Testament* has one goal to accomplish: to demonstrate "that every chronological statement contained in the Sacred Writ is consistent with all other chronological statements contained therein." The author carefully and thoroughly investigates the chronological and mathematical facts of the Old Testament, proving them to be accurate and reliable. This biblically sound, scholarly, and easy-to-understand book will enlighten and astound its readers with solutions and alternatives to many questions Bible scholars have had over the centuries.

8 1/2 x 11 • 300 pages
Hardcover • ISBN:0-89051-416-X
$24.99

REFERENCE

Features:

- Solution to the chronology of Judges
- Solution to Daniel 9:25, the 483-year prophecy
- Solution to the length of the Hebrews' sojourn in Egypt
- Solution to the "number of souls" in Egypt when Jacob came there
- Chronology of the life of Christ

- Chronology of the kings of the divided monarchy
- 48 charts, graphs, and diagrams
- Fully indexed/complete bibliography
- Major revision over previous editions with numerous additional documentation, references, and 14 new technical appendixes

Serves as a powerful apologetics tool for colleges and seminaries.

Available at Christian bookstores nationwide
FIND OTHER GREAT TITLES AT WWW.MASTERBOOKS.NET

THE ANNALS OF THE WORLD

JAMES USSHER

Considered not only a literary classic, but also an accurate historical reference from creation to A.D. 70, *The Annals of the World* has, for the first time, been translated into modern English from the original Latin text. This treasure-trove of material also contains many human interest stories from the original historical documents collected by devoted Christian historian and scholar Archbishop James Ussher. Precisely dated and referenced, this is more than just a fascinating history book — it's a work of history.

8 3/8 x 10 7/8 • 960 pages
Hardcover • ISBN: 0-89051-360-0
$69.99

GENERAL INTEREST/ GENERAL TOPIC/ HISTORY

Features:

- Over 2,500 citations from the Bible and the Apocrypha
- Ussher's original citations have been checked against the latest textual scholarship
- A one-of-a-kind reference book for every library
- Smythe-sewn with gold-gilded edges and foil embossed
- Beautiful display box included
- 8 appendices with over 10,000 original footnotes
- Includes supplemental reference CD-ROM

This is the first English translation of this enormously important work in over 300 years!

Available at Christian bookstores nationwide
FIND OTHER GREAT TITLES AT WWW.MASTERBOOKS.NET

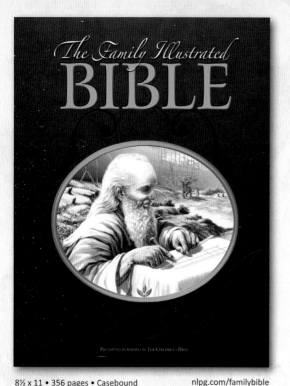

The Family Illustrated BIBLE

Previously published as The Children's Bible

8½ x 11 • 356 pages • Casebound
Retail: $24.99 U.S.
ISBN 13: 978-0-89221-704-5

BIBLES / New International Version / General
RELIGION / Biblical Studies / History & Culture

nlpg.com/familybible

An inspiring, insightful, and exquisitely rendered presentation of the Bible!

See the people, culture, and events of the Bible come to vibrant life through images and detailed biblical accounts from the *New International Version*.

Examine God's covenants, a detailed map of the lands of the Bible, clear timelines, and facts about the people found within the pages of Scripture, along with a thorough index. *The Family Illustrated Bible* will become a household treasure, inspiring generations to come.

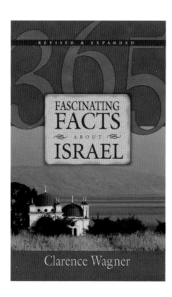
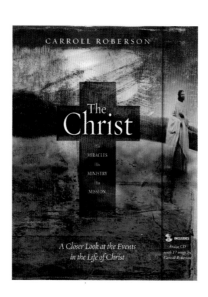

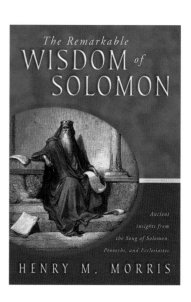

Join the
Conversation

Ask the experts

Build relationships

Share your thoughts

Download free resources

Creation
Conversations
.com

This is your invitation to our
online community of believers.

Learn

Teach

Share

Join the
Biblical Archaeology Group
TODAY!

Biblical Archaeology

http://www.creationconversations.com/group/biblicalarchaeologywatch

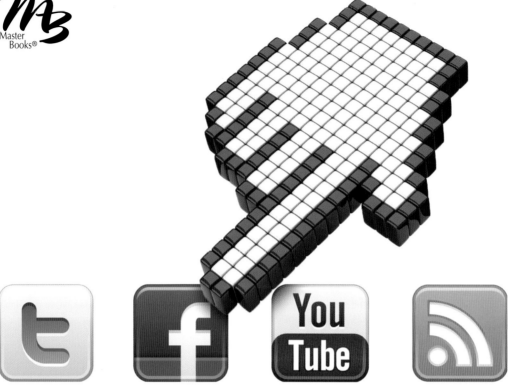

Connect with Master Books®

masterbooks.net   An Imprint of New Leaf Publishing Group

facebook.com/**masterbooks**
twitter.com/**masterbooks4u**
youtube.com/**nlpgvideo**

nlpgblogs.com
nlpgvideos.com

Connect with author David Down

www.diggings.com.au